Circle Time From A to Z

More Than 180 Alphabet Activities for Group Time

- Beginning sounds
- Letter-sound association
- Letter recognition
- Letter identification
- Uppercase letters
- Lowercase letters
- Letter formation
- Ending sounds
- and MORE!

Managing Editor: Kelly Robertson

Editorial Team: Becky S. Andrews, Margaret Aumen, Diane Badden, Pamela Ballingal, Amy Brinton, Tricia Brown, Kimberley Bruck, Karen A. Brudnak, Marie E. Cecchini, Pam Crane, Chris Curry, Kathryn Davenport, Roxanne LaBell Dearman, Lynn Drolet, Shanda Fitte, Sarah Foreman, Pierce Foster, Kate Franzmann, Kathy Ginn, Ada Goren, Karen Guess, Tazmen Hansen, Marsha Heim, Lori Z. Henry, Kim Hintze, Debra Liverman, Kitty Lowrance, Beth Marquardt, Brenda Miner, Jennifer Nunn, Tina Petersen, Gerri Primak, Mark Rainey, Greg D. Rieves, Hope Rodgers, Rebecca Saunders, Alicia K. Shaffer, Betty Silkunas, Leanne Stratton Swinson, Donna K. Teal, Rachael Traylor, Sharon M. Tresino, Susan Walker, Carole Watkins, Zane Williard, Joyce Wilson

www.themailbox.com

©2010 The Mailbox® Books
All rights reserved.
ISBN10 #1-56234-954-6 • ISBN13 #978-1-56234-954-7

Except as provided for herein, no part of this publication may be reproduced or transmitted in any form or by any means, electronic or mechanical, including photocopying, recording, or storing in any information storage and retrieval system or electronic online bulletin board, without prior written permission from The Education Center, Inc. Permission is given to the original purchaser to reproduce patterns and reproducibles for individual classroom use only and not for resale or distribution. Reproduction for an entire school or school system is prohibited. Please direct written inquiries to The Education Center, Inc., P.O. Box 9753, Greensboro, NC 27429-0753. The Education Center®, The Mailbox®, the mailbox/post/grass logo, and The Mailbox Book Company® are registered trademarks of The Education Center, Inc. All other brand or product names are trademarks or registered trademarks of their respective companies.

Printed in the United States
10 9 8 7 6 5 4 3 2 1

HPS 215499

Table of Contents

What's Inside 3

A	 4
B	 8
C	 12
D	 16
E	 20
F	 24
G	 28
H	 32
I	 36
J	 40
K	 44
L	 48
M	 52
N	 56
O	 60
P	 64
Q	 68
R	 70
S	 74
T	 78
U	 82
V	 84
W	 86
X	 90
Y	 92
Z	 94

Patterns and More 96

What's Inside

Circle-time activities for *every* alphabet letter!

Patterns and More

Pocketful of A

Beginning sound /ā/

Model the apron for the group and guide students to hear the /ā/ sound at the beginning of *apron.* Next, ask each child to put on a pretend apron. Explain that the apron has a large front pocket for holding objects that begin like *apron.* Then name and describe different items that begin with /ā/ *(acorn, ape, angel, aphid)* and some that do not. After each description, ask, "Does it go in your apron pocket?" When the answer is yes, each child pretends to tuck the object in her apron pocket. When the answer is no, each child shakes her index finger to further emphasize the response.

Materials:
apron with a large front pocket

To get ready:
Put on the apron.

Blastoff!

Beginning sound /ă/

Youngsters take the controls as junior astronauts during this activity! Have each astronaut sit and position her hands to make a small rocket ship. Emphasize the beginning /ă/ sound of *astronaut* and explain to students that, as astronauts, they launch their rocket ships only when a flight name begins like *astronaut.* For a test flight, announce "Flight Apple" and demonstrate how to launch and fly a rocket from a seated position. Then continue with a series of flight names, most of which begin with the /ă/ sound.

Materials:
none

To get ready:
No preparation is necessary.

Circle Time From A to Z • ©The Mailbox® Books • TEC61276

Song and Dance
Letter-sound association

Invite little ones to stand. Give each child a card and then lead youngsters in singing and performing this fun twist on a favorite song and dance. Emphasize the /ă/ sound throughout the performance.

Materials:
class supply of blank cards

To get ready:
Label each card with an *A*.

(sung to the tune of "The Hokey-Pokey")

I put my *A* in.
I put my *A* out.
I put my *A* in,
And I shake it all about.
I hold it by my nose,
And then I hold it by my toes.
That's how the *A* song goes.

I show my *A* to myself.
I show my *A* to you.
I show my *A* to myself,
And I shake it—one, two.
I hold it by my nose,
And then I hold it by my toes.
That's how the *A* song goes.

A Is for Apple
Letter-sound association

Review the /ă/ sound with little ones, using the apple as a prop. Then, on the chart, draw and label a simple picture of an apple as shown. Next, invite volunteers to name other objects that begin with /ă/. Draw and label a simple picture of each object, each time linking the /ă/ sound to the letter *A*. If desired, repeat this activity for the /ā/ sound.

Materials:
apple
large sheet of chart paper
markers

To get ready:
Write *Aa* at the top of the paper.

Picking Apples
Letter recognition

Materials:
several die-cut apples
large tree cutout or outline
small basket

To get ready:
Label the apples with letters, writing *A* on most. Place the tree on the floor and display the apples on the tree. Set the basket nearby.

Lead the group in saying the chant. Then invite a volunteer to pick an apple labeled with the letter *A*. Ask her to show the letter to the group before she puts the apple in the basket. Continue the apple-picking process, repeating the chant each time, until all the apples labeled with *A* are picked.

Apples, apples,
Look and see.
Pick an *A*
From the tree.

Hungry Alligators
Letter identification

Materials:
pointer

To get ready:
Write letters on the board, making sure to include several *A*s.

Show students how to use their hands to make alligator mouths. Then ask each child to pretend she is a hungry alligator that is ready for a snack of *A*s. Point in random order to the letters on the board. When the letter is an *A*, students respond, "Yum! Letter *A!*" and quickly open and close their alligator mouths. When the letter is not an *A*, the students shake their heads to indicate no.

Gathering Acorns
Uppercase and lowercase letters

Have little ones pretend to be squirrels. Next, select a few volunteers to each gather an acorn as you lead the waiting squirrels in chanting the rhyme. When a child finds an acorn, he stands near the basket with the matching letter. Then, on your cue, each volunteer shows his acorn to his classmates and places it in the basket. If desired, have the waiting squirrels make chatter noises to show their approval. Continue with different volunteers.

Little squirrels, look around.
Find an acorn on the ground.

Materials:
class supply of acorn cutouts
2 blank cards
2 small baskets

To get ready:
Label one blank card *A* and the other *a*; attach each card to a different basket. Then label each acorn either *A* or *a* for sorting. Scatter the acorns.

A Stylish Hat
Medial /ă/

Invite a volunteer to take a card from the gift bag and name its picture. Help the group decide whether the name shares a sound with the word *hat*. (All the pictures' names share the /ă/ sound.) Then have the child say the shared sound and place the card on the hat. Continue until all the cards are on display. Then have students study the cards to determine which letter in each word makes the /ă/ sound.

Materials:
medial /ă/ picture cards (page 96)
extra large hat cutout
gift bag

To get ready:
Cut apart a copy of the picture cards and place them in the gift bag.

Bb

Fill the Basket
Beginning sound /b/

Set the basket on the floor and give each youngster an object. Have each child, in turn, name her item. If it begins with the /b/ sound, she puts it in the basket. If it does not, she places the item in a discard pile. After each child takes her turn, remove individual items from the basket. Join youngsters in naming each item, giving extra emphasis to its beginning sound.

Materials:
large basket
classroom items, most of whose names begin with /b/

To get ready:
No preparation is necessary.

Round the Bases
Beginning sound /b/

Place the bear on home plate. Call out words, making sure some of the words begin with the /b/ sound. When youngsters hear a word that begins with /b/, they call out, "Next base, bear!" emphasizing each /b/ sound. Then invite a volunteer to move the bear to first base. Continue the activity, inviting different volunteers to move the bear around the bases until it reaches home plate.

Materials:
stuffed bear
4 sheets of construction paper

To get ready:
Arrange the paper on the floor to represent home plate and first, second, and third bases.

A Puffy B
Letter-sound association

Announce a variety of words, most of them beginning with the /b/ sound. Each time a youngster hears a word that begins with /b/, he places a pom-pom on his letter *B*. Continue naming words in this manner until each child has covered his letter *B* with pom-poms.

Materials:
construction paper square labeled with the letter *B* for each child
generous supply of pom-poms

To get ready:
Give each child a sheet of paper and a handful of pom-poms.

Beach Ball Bounce
Letter-sound association

Bounce the beach ball to a student. Then invite her to say a word whose name begins with /b/. After confirming her answer, have her bounce the ball to a classmate. Continue until each child has had a turn.

Materials:
beach ball

To get ready:
Label the ball with a large *B*.

Hear Them Ring!
Letter recognition

Give each child a jingle bell and ask him to hold it in his lap. Hold a card in the air. If the letter on the card is *B*, students ring their bells. If it is not, the youngsters keep their bells still.

Materials:
class supply of large jingle bells
blank cards

To get ready:
Label each card with a letter, writing *B* on most.

Is It a B?
Letter recognition

Give each child a sticky note and have him decide whether the letter on his note is a *B*. Then invite three or four students at a time to place their notes on the corresponding section of the paper.

Materials:
large piece of paper
sticky notes

To get ready:
Label the paper as shown. Program a class supply of sticky notes with letters, writing the letter *B* on most notes.

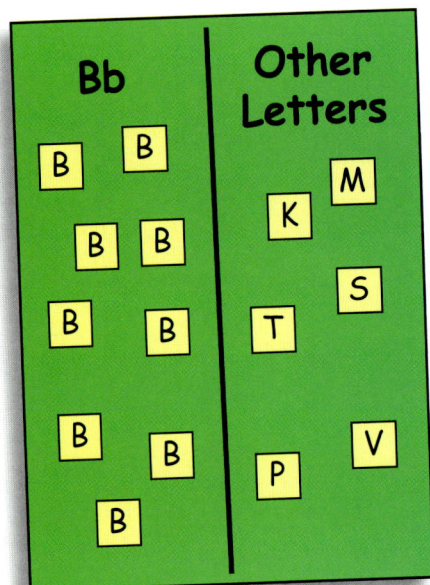

Bears and Honeypots
Uppercase and lowercase letters

Give each child a honeypot cutout. Have each youngster, in turn, decide whether the letter on her honeypot is an uppercase or a lowercase *B*. After confirming her answer, have the child place the honeypot near the appropriate bear.

Materials:
large stuffed bear
small stuffed bear
class supply of honeypot cutouts

To get ready:
Label the cutouts with *B* or *b*. Label the bears as shown.

Busy Bees
Uppercase and lowercase letters

Give the bag to a child and start the music. Instruct students to pass the bag around the circle while the music is playing. Periodically stop the music, signaling youngsters to freeze. Have the child holding the bag remove a bee, identify the letter, and place it on the appropriate beehive. Then restart the music.

Materials:
class supply of bee cutouts (page 112)
2 large beehive cutouts
gift bag
music player
music

To get ready:
Store the bees in the bag.

Tray of Cookies
Beginning sound /k/

Invite a child to turn over a cookie and name the picture shown. Ask the group to decide whether the name begins with the hard *c* sound like *cookie*. If it does, the child leaves the cookie faceup on the tray. If it does not, the child removes the cookie from the tray and sets it aside.

Materials:
class supply of cookie cutouts (page 97)
baking tray

To get ready:
Put the cookies picture-side down on the tray.

If It Starts With...
Beginning sound /k/

Announce a word. Then lead youngsters in singing the song. If the word begins with the hard *c* sound, students clap their hands at the appropriate times during the song. If the word begins with a different sound, youngsters keep their hands still.

Materials:
none

To get ready:
No preparation is necessary.

(sung to the tune of
"If You're Happy and You Know It")

If [car] begins with /k/, clap your hands.
If [car] begins with /k/, clap your hands.
If [car] begins with /k/,
Use your hands to show you know it.
If [car] begins with /k/, clap your hands.

Cc Cc Cc Cc Cc Cc Cc Cc Cc Cc Cc

Layer Cake
Letter-sound association

Identify the letter *C* and tell youngsters you need their help in making several more layers for this cake. Then invite a volunteer to name a word that begins with the hard *c* sound like *cake*. (Encourage him to ask the group for assistance if needed.) After confirming his answer, ask the child to draw another layer on the cake. Continue in the same way with different volunteers to make a multilayer cake.

Materials:
none

To get ready:
Draw on the board a plate with a one-layer cake labeled with a *C*.

Cucumber Picking
Letter recognition

Have each child, in turn, flip a cucumber and decide whether the letter on it is a *C*. If it is, he leaves the cucumber on the vine. If it is not, he removes the cucumber from the vine and sets it aside.

Materials:
class supply of green ovals (cucumbers)
green yarn

To get ready:
Label each cutout with a letter, writing *C* on most. Lay a length of yarn (vine) on the floor. Place the cucumbers along the vine letter-side down.

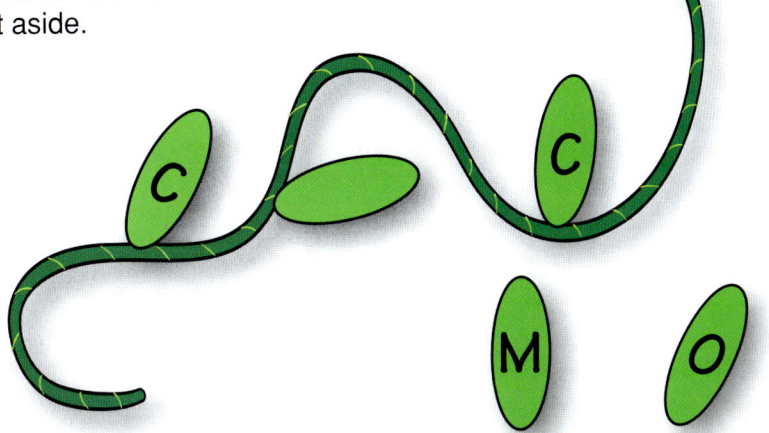

Cc Cc Cc Cc Cc Cc Cc Cc Cc

Circle Time From A to Z • ©The Mailbox® Books • TEC61276

Cc Cc Cc Cc Cc Cc Cc Cc Cc Cc Cc

Materials:
2 equal sets of blank cards

To get ready:
Label each card in one set with *C* and each card in the remaining set with a different letter. Stack the sets in separate piles with the cards facedown.

Ready, Aim, Click!
Letter recognition

Display one card from each pile and ask the group to decide which card is labeled with the letter *C*. Have students pretend to point a camera at the appropriate card as you lead them in saying the rhyme. At the end of the rhyme, each child pretends to take a picture of the *C*. Repeat with the remaining cards.

I spy the letter *C*.
Take a picture—one, two, three!

Materials:
empty cake mix box
plastic mixing bowl
mixing spoon
several letter manipulatives, most of which are *C*

To get ready:
Put the letters in the box. Set out the bowl and spoon.

Stir the Batter
Letter identification

To make this letter *C* cake batter, have a child remove a letter from the box and ask the group to identify it. If the letter is a *C*, the child puts it in the bowl and stirs it around as you lead the group in singing the song. If it is a different letter, she sets it aside.

(sung to the tune of "Row, Row, Row Your Boat")

Stir, stir, stir the batter.
Stir it round and round.
Just the right ingredient
Is the letter *C* you found!

Cc Cc Cc Cc Cc Cc Cc Cc Cc

Carrot Patch
Uppercase and lowercase letters

Have each child, in turn, pick a carrot and name whether the letter is uppercase or lowercase. After confirming his answer, have the child put the carrot in the appropriate colander.

Materials:
2 colanders (or colander-shaped cutouts)
class supply of carrot cutouts
length of brown paper (garden)

To get ready:
Label each carrot cutout with either an uppercase or a lowercase *C*. Place the carrots facedown on the garden. Label the colanders as shown. Place them near the garden.

Hungry Cats
Letter formation

Give each child a programmed paper and a cat. Have each student place her cat at the beginning of the letter. Ring the bell and say, "Here, kitty, kitty! It's time to eat!" Each child moves her cat along the letter toward the dish. After pretending the cat nibbles on the food, each youngster returns her cat to the beginning of the letter to repeat the activity.

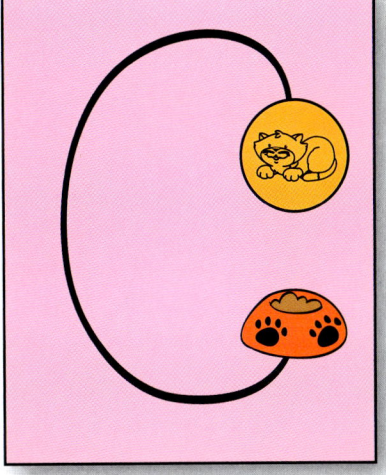

Materials:
class supply of construction paper
class supply of cat cutouts (If desired, use the cat pattern from page 97.)
bell

To get ready:
Program the construction paper with *C* and a food dish as shown.

Dd

Time to Dust!
Beginning sound /d/

Use the feather duster to dust the doll as you lead the group in saying, "Dust, dust, dust that dusty [doll]," emphasizing each /d/ sound. Then hand the duster to a volunteer and invite her to dust an object in the room whose name begins the same as *doll*. As she begins to dust an object, lead students in repeating the sentence, substituting the name of the new object for *doll*. Continue until each child has had a turn.

Materials:
feather duster
doll

To get ready:
No preparation is necessary.

Pick the Picture
Beginning sound /d/

Place three pictures in the pocket chart, making sure that at least one picture's name begins with /d/. Then secretly choose one of the pictures and give the group two clues about the picture: one clue about its beginning sound and one general clue (similar to the ones shown). Invite a volunteer to name the picture. Lead the group in repeating the name of the pictured item, emphasizing its beginning sound. Continue in the described manner using different groups of pictures.

Materials:
pictures, most of whose names begin with /d/
pocket chart

To get ready:
No preparation is necessary.

Its name begins like door.
It is something you can eat.

Where Is D?
Letter-sound association

Using two of the puppets, sing and perform the song below for students. Then invite three volunteers to each take two puppets and help you lead the class in singing the song again. Repeat the song until each child has had a turn using the puppets.

(sung to the tune of "Where Is Thumbkin?")

Where is *D*? Where is *D*?	Hold puppets behind back.
Here I am! Here I am!	Hold up one puppet and then the other.
Can you say the *D* sound?	Wiggle one puppet.
Can you say the *D* sound?	Wiggle the other puppet.
/d/, /d/, /d/,	Wiggle both puppets.
/d/, /d/, /d/.	

Materials:
eight duck cutouts (patterns on page 98)
eight craft sticks
tape

To get ready:
Label each duck with a *D*. Then tape a craft stick to the back of each duck.

Ding-Dong
Letter-sound association

Invite a volunteer to ring the doorbell. Lead the group in saying, "Ding-dong! Ding-dong! What's behind our *D* door?" emphasizing each /d/ sound. Then ask a question containing the picture's name and a rhyming word, such as "Is it a dog or a log?" Invite the volunteer to name the picture and then open the door to check his answer. Secretly change pictures to repeat the activity.

Materials:
pictures whose names begin with /d/
large sheet of tagboard

To get ready:
Prepare a door like the one shown. Post the door and place one picture behind it. Set the other pictures nearby.

Dd Dd Dd Dd Dd Dd Dd Dd Dd Dd Dd

Does It Have a D?
Letter recognition

Invite a volunteer to remove a card from the bag and show it to the class. Have the group read the name on the card. Then enlist students' help in determining whether a *D* (or *d*) is in the name. If it is, write the name on the dog, highlighting the appropriate letter(s). If the name does not contain a *D* or *d*, have the child set the card aside. Continue with the remaining cards.

Materials:
large dog cutout
class supply of blank cards
paper lunch bag

To get ready:
Label the dog "Dd." Write each child's name on a card and place it in the bag. Post the dog and set the bag nearby.

Dots for Dinosaur
Letter identification

Have a child point to a sticky note labeled with a *D* and identify it. Direct the group to say, "Dinosaur gets a dot," emphasizing each /d/ sound. Then have the child remove the sticky note and use the bingo dauber to add a dot to the dinosaur. Continue with the remaining sticky notes labeled with *D*s. To conclude, invite the youngsters to confirm that the remaining sticky notes are not labeled with *D*s and have students remove them.

Materials:
large dinosaur cutout (pattern on page 98)
small sticky notes
bingo daubers

To get ready:
Label each sticky note with a letter, writing a *D* on most. Post the dinosaur in a student-accessible location. Attach the sticky notes to the dinosaur and set the bingo daubers nearby.

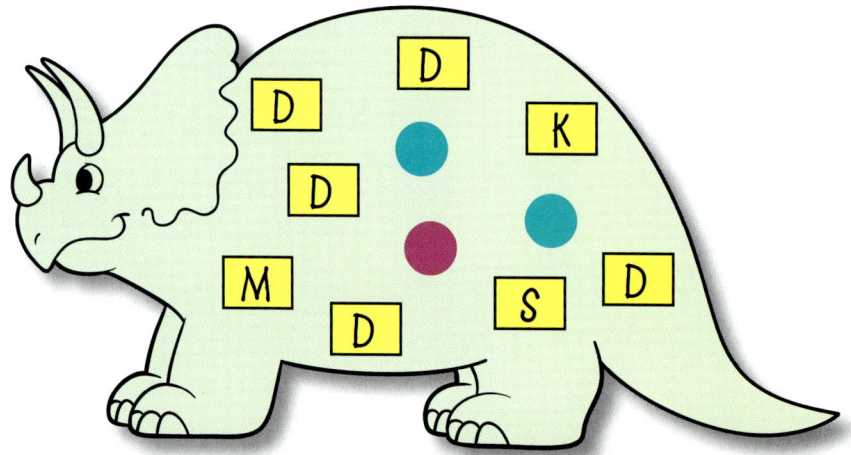

Dd Dd Dd Dd Dd Dd Dd Dd Dd

Darling Ducks
Uppercase and lowercase letters

Invite a youngster to choose a duckling labeled with a *d* and place it in the pond. Direct students to verify that the duckling is labeled with *d* and say, "Quack, quack!" to show their approval. Continue until all the ducks labeled with *d* have been placed in the pond with their mother.

Materials:
large duck cutout (enlarge a pattern on page 98)
class supply of small duck cutouts (patterns on page 98)
large pond cutout

To get ready:
Label the large duck with a *D*. Program each small duck with a lowercase letter, writing *d* on most. Place the large duck (mother duck) in the pond and arrange the small ducks (ducklings) around the pond.

The Doctor Is In
Letter formation

Have students imagine that they are doctors. Then tell the group that the *D*s have had an accident and the students need to help fix them. Have each child remove a piece of a *D* from the bag. Then have each youngster find a classmate with a piece needed to mend his *D*. Invite the pair to mend the *D* by gluing it to the paper. If desired, repeat the activity using *d*'s.

Materials:
D cutout for every two students (Plan to participate if you have an odd number of students.)
length of bulletin board paper
toy doctor's bag
glue

To get ready:
Cut each *D* into two pieces: a straight piece and a curved piece. Place the pieces in the doctor's bag. Label the paper as shown and set it out.

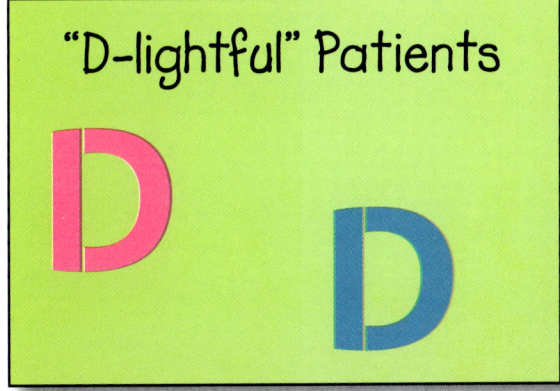

Ee Ee Ee Ee Ee Ee Ee Ee Ee Ee Ee Ee

E Like Eagle
Beginning sound /ē/

Lead youngsters in singing the song shown. Next, ask a volunteer to name a word that begins with /ē/ like *eagle*. Then have her take the eagle puppet and "fly" it around the circle as the class sings the song again. Continue as time permits. **For a short *e* variation,** sing /ĕ/ instead of /ē/ in the song and have the volunteer pretend to be an elephant.

Materials:
eagle pattern (page 99)
craft stick
tape

To get ready:
Cut out a copy of the eagle pattern and tape it to a craft stick to make a puppet.

(sung to the tune of "The Farmer in the Dell")

One sound of *E* is /ē/.
One sound of *E* is /ē/.
Heigh-ho, oh, did you know
One sound of *E* is /ē/?

Materials:
none

To get ready:
No preparation is necessary.

Elbow.

Swinging Trunks
Beginning sound /ĕ/

Have youngsters imagine that they are elephants who get excited when they hear words that begin with /ĕ/ like *elephant.* Then name a word. If it begins with /ĕ/, have each child clasp his hands and swing his arms in front of him so they resemble an elephant's trunk. If it begins with a different sound, direct each student to remain still. Continue naming words as time allows.

Ee Ee Ee Ee Ee Ee Ee Ee Ee Ee Ee Ee

All Aboard the E Trains
Letter matching

Invite two students to imagine they are train engines. Give each engine a different letter cutout. Give each remaining youngster a card at random. Tell each engine to hold his letter cutout overhead as he "chugs" around the room. Then invite each child to match her card's letter to a letter cutout and "chug" behind the corresponding engine, pretending to be a train car. After checking for accuracy, have each train return to a predetermined location (train station). If desired, collect and redistribute the letter cutouts and cards to form new trains.

Materials:
large uppercase *E* cutout
large lowercase *e* cutout
class supply of blank cards

To get ready:
On half the cards, write an uppercase *E.* Write a lowercase *e* on each remaining card. Shuffle the cards.

Eggs in the Basket
Letter recognition

Tell youngsters that you need their help collecting eggs for a special recipe. Have the children each find an egg and then gather around the basket. Explain that only the eggs labeled with *E* can be used in the recipe. Then have each child holding an *E* egg place it in the basket and each youngster holding an egg labeled with a different letter set it aside.

Materials:
class supply of egg cutouts
basket

To get ready:
Label each egg with a letter, writing *E* on most. Place the eggs around the room in clearly visible locations.

Let's Eat!
Letter recognition

Show a letter card. If a child sees the letter *E*, he pretends to eat his favorite food. If he sees any other letter, he shakes his head. Continue with each remaining card.

Materials:
several blank cards

To get ready:
Label each card with a letter, writing *E* on most.

Seeking *E*s
Letter identification

After reading aloud a sentence from the paper, invite a child to take the crayon and pretend to be an eagle. Then have him "fly" to the chart and use his keen eagle eyes to find and identify an *E*. After confirming he is correct, have him circle the letter before passing the crayon to a classmate. Continue as time permits.

Materials:
chart paper
several feathers
crayon
tape

To get ready:
Write several sentences with multiple *E*s on the chart paper. Tape the feathers to the crayon.

Eva Eagle lives in Elkton, Oregon.

Eva Eagle has a very big beak!

Eva has a brother named Elliot Eagle.

Egg Pairs
Uppercase and lowercase letters

Have each youngster crack an egg open, look at his letter, and determine whether he has an uppercase or a lowercase *E*. Then instruct students to walk around, look at each other's letters, and form uppercase and lowercase letter pairs. (If a child gets the bonus egg, he walks around the room as a helper.) Each time a match is made, have partners sit down and wait for you to check their letters. For another round, challenge each child to form a letter pair with a different partner.

Materials:
class supply of plastic eggs
class supply of paper squares

To get ready:
Write *E* on half the paper squares and *e* on the other half. (If there is an odd number, write *Ee* on the last square to make a bonus egg.) Put one square in each egg.

Elf Helpers
Letter formation

To help this elf form solid-colored *E*s, have each child remove a strip from the bag as it is passed around the circle. Then guide youngsters to form groups based on the color of their strips. Instruct each group to use its strips to form an uppercase *E*. For groups with fewer than four children, have the group members return to the elf bag to find the missing strips before forming the letter *E*. After checking each *E* for accuracy, have youngsters return the strips to the bag and repeat the activity.

Materials:
elf card (page 99)
class supply (or more) of paper strips, 4 strips per color
paper bag
tape

To get ready:
Color and cut out the elf card; then tape it to the bag. Put all the strips in the bag.

A Fishy Pond
Beginning sound /f/

Have each child, in turn, flip a fish and name the pictured item. If the name begins with /f/, the child drops the fish in the pail. If it does not, he puts the fish beside the pail. When the pond is empty, remove each fish from the pail. Lead youngsters to name each picture, emphasizing each /f/ sound.

Materials:
pond cutout
class supply of fish cutouts
pictures, most of whose
   names begin with *f*
pail
glue

To get ready:
Glue a picture on each fish cutout. Put the fish picture-side down on the pond. Set the pail nearby.

Football Handoff
Beginning sound /f/

Give the football to a child and start the music. Instruct youngsters to pass the football around the circle while the music is playing. Periodically stop the music to signal students to freeze. Announce two words: one that begins like *football* and one that does not. The child holding the football names the word that has the beginning sound /f/. After confirming his answer, have the class repeat the word, emphasizing the /f/ sound. Then restart the music.

Materials:
football
music player
music

To get ready:
No preparation is necessary.

Flashlight Fun
Letter-sound association

Materials:
several flashlights
large letter *F* sign

To get ready:
Post the sign. Turn on each flashlight. Dim the classroom lights.

Give each flashlight to a different volunteer and ask her to hold it upside down in her lap. Announce a word. Ask the group to decide whether the word begins with the /f/ sound. If it does, each child holding a flashlight shines the light on the letter *F*. If it does not, the youngsters keep their flashlights still. After announcing two or three words, pause to allow each flashlight holder to hand her light to a classmate.

Block by Block
Letter-sound association

Demonstrate how to make an *F* by tracing the letter on the sign with your finger. Then invite a volunteer to say a word that begins with the /f/ sound. Lead the group in saying the word; then have the child place a block on the floor. Continue with other volunteers until the letter *F* is formed with the blocks.

Materials:
rectangular blocks
large letter *F* sign

To get ready:
No preparation is necessary.

Materials:
several blank cards
class supply of feathers

To get ready:
Label each card with a letter, writing *F* on most.

Tickle Time
Letter recognition

Give each child a feather to hold in his lap. Hold a card up. When the letter is an *F*, youngsters tickle their faces with the feathers. When the letter is not *F*, they hold their feathers still.

Materials:
several blank cards
empty picture frame

To get ready:
Label each card with a letter, writing *F* on most. Stack the cards facedown.

Funny Faces
Letter identification

Invite a volunteer to take and hold up a card. Ask the group to identify the letter. When the letter is *F*, the group says, "Funny face!" The volunteer then looks through the picture frame and makes a funny face. Her classmates imitate her expression. When the letter is not *F*, her turn is over.

Fluttering Fireflies
Uppercase and lowercase letters

Name the letter on each jar, specifying whether it's uppercase or lowercase. Then invite a volunteer to take a card, identify the letter, and place the card on the appropriate jar. If he puts the card on the correct jar, his classmates flutter their fingers (fireflies) in the air. If he does not, they hold their fingers still.

Materials:
firefly cards (page 100)
2 large jar cutouts
scissors

To get ready:
Cut out the firefly cards and stack them facedown. Label the jar cutouts as shown.

Fabulous Feathers
Uppercase and lowercase letters

Instruct each child to find one feather. After each student identifies the letter on her feather, lead the group in saying the rhyme. Then help each child attach her feather to the turkey.

Poor Mr. Turkey!
He's not ready for cold weather.
Let's get him dressed
With our letter *F* feathers!

Materials:
turkey body cutout
class supply of construction paper feathers
Sticky-Tac or tape

To get ready:
Program the feathers with *F* or *f*. Place the feathers around the room in plain sight and display the turkey on a wall.

Gorilla Play
Beginning sound /g/

Have a student choose an item and say its name. Ask youngsters to decide whether the name begins like *gorilla*. If it does, the child places the item near the gorilla and then leads the group in performing gorillalike sounds and actions. If it does not, he sets the item aside.

Materials:
toy gorilla (or picture of one) several objects or pictures of objects, most of whose names begin with the hard *g* sound

To get ready:
Set out the gorilla. Place the items nearby.

Good Going!
Beginning sound /g/

Secretly think of a word that begins with the hard *g* sound. Then give students a clue about the word and invite a volunteer to guess the word. Continue to give clues until a student correctly guesses the word. Then give a thumbs-up and lead youngsters in saying, "Good going!" emphasizing each hard *g* sound.

Materials:
none

To get ready:
No preparation is necessary.

Colorful Gumballs
Letter-sound association

Announce two or three words, making sure one of the words begins with the hard *g* sound. Then ask a volunteer to tell which of the words begins like *gumball*. After confirming her answer, have her remove a gumball from the board. Continue until each child has had a turn and the gumball machine is empty.

Materials:
class supply of colorful construction paper circles
tape

To get ready:
Draw a large gumball machine on the board. Label the paper circles with *G*s. Put rolled tape on the back of each circle to attach it to the board.

Can You Find...
Letter-sound association

Identify the letter *G* on the card. Then ask a volunteer to study the picture cards while you lead the remaining youngsters in singing the song. At the end of the song, the student selects a picture of an item whose name begins with the hard *g* sound, announces the word, and places the card in the pocket chart. Continue until all the appropriate cards are in the chart.

Materials:
beginning sound picture cards (page 101)
letter *G* card
pocket chart

To get ready:
Cut out a copy of the picture cards. Spread them out faceup on the floor. Display the letter card in the pocket chart.

(sung to the tune of "The Muffin Man")

Oh, find a picture that starts with /g/,
That starts with /g/, that starts with /g/.
Oh, find a picture that starts with /g/,
The sound of letter *G*.

Miniature Golf
Letter recognition

Give each child a putting green, a golf ball, and a golf club. To begin, have her put the golf ball on the tee. Then hold up a card. If the card is labeled with a *G*, each youngster uses her golf club to putt the ball to the hole. If the card is labeled with a different letter, she holds her golf club still.

Materials:
several blank cards
class supply of pom-poms (golf balls)
class supply of green construction paper (putting greens)
class supply of jumbo craft sticks (golf clubs)

To get ready:
Label each card with a letter, writing *G* on most. Program each putting green with a small dot (golf tee) and a circle (hole) labeled as shown.

Where Is G?
Letter identification

Instruct students to close their eyes. Place the *G* on the board. Have youngsters open their eyes and put on imaginary goggles, as shown, to help them find the *G*. When a child finds *G*, he calls out, "*G* is for *goggles!*" Then he points to the letter and says its name. If he is correct, youngsters close their eyes again as you move the *G* to another location on the board. If he is incorrect, help him correctly identify the *G* before changing its location.

Materials:
magnetic board
several magnetic letters, including one *G*

To get ready:
Place the letters, except *G*, on the board.

In the Garbage
Uppercase and lowercase letters

Ask each youngster to help clean the room by finding one labeled paper scrap and bringing it to the circle. Each student tells the group whether the letter on her paper scrap is an uppercase or a lowercase *G*. Then she puts the scrap in the appropriate garbage can.

Materials:
2 small plastic garbage cans
class supply of large paper scraps

To get ready:
Label each paper scrap with an uppercase or a lowercase *G*. Place the scraps around the room where they can be easily found. Set out the garbage cans, labeled as shown.

Does It End Like *Rug*?
Ending sound /g/

Invite a child to take a card and hold it in the air. Have students name the picture shown. If the name ends like *rug*, the child places the card on the rug. If it does not, he sets the card aside. After all the cards have been taken from the stack, remove each card from the rug, in turn, and lead youngsters in naming the picture again, placing extra emphasis on each ending sound.

Materials:
ending sound picture cards (page 102)
small throw rug

To get ready:
Set out the rug. Stack the cards facedown nearby.

Hh

Hot Hands
Beginning sound /h/

Have each youngster hold his hands in front of his mouth. Say the /h/ sound and have students repeat it several times. Guide students to notice that they feel their breath on their hands when they say the /h/ sound. One at a time, announce words, most of which begin with /h/. When students hear a word that begins with /h/, they hold their hands in front of their mouths and make the /h/ sound. If they hear a word that begins with a different sound, they keep their hands at their sides.

Materials:
none

To get ready:
No preparation is necessary.

"Happy."

Hay Is for Horses
Beginning sound /h/

Invite a volunteer to choose a haystack and name the picture. If the name begins with /h/, the group says, "Hay is for horses," as the child places the haystack near the horse. If the name begins with a different sound, the group says nothing and the volunteer sets the haystack aside.

Materials:
class supply of picture cards (page 103)
horse cutout (page 103)
class supply of haystack cutouts
glue

To get ready:
Glue a card to each haystack and place the haystacks facedown. Set the horse nearby.

Hide-and-Seek
Letter-sound association

Tell youngsters they are looking for a sneaky *H* that is hiding behind a picture whose name begins with /h/. Invite a volunteer to name a picture whose name begins with /h/. Remove the picture from the pocket chart and have students check to see whether the *H* is behind it. Continue in this manner until the *H* is revealed. For another round, hide the *H* card behind a different picture whose name begins with /h/.

Materials:
picture cards (page 103)
13 blank cards
pocket chart
glue

To get ready:
Glue each picture card to a different blank card and place the cards faceup in a pocket chart. Label the remaining blank card with *H*. Put it behind a picture card whose name begins with /h/.

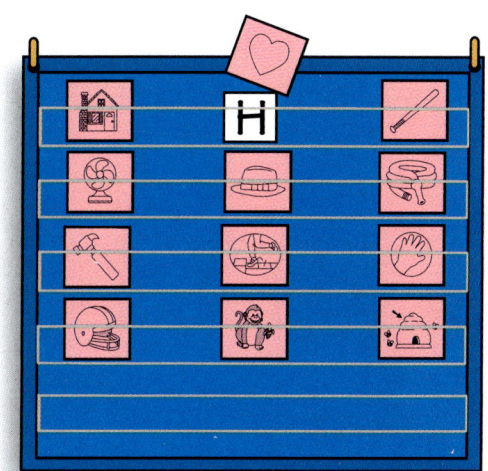

Happy Hearts
Letter-sound association

Give each child a heart. Name a word. If the word begins with /h/, direct students to hold up their hearts as they say, "Happy hearts!" emphasizing each /h/ sound. If the word begins with a different sound, direct the group to do nothing. Repeat the process several times using different words.

Materials:
class supply of heart cutouts

To get ready:
On each heart, draw a happy face with an *H* for a nose.

Give a Cheer
Letter recognition

Invite little ones to pretend they are cheerleaders who are cheering for the *H* team. Show the group a letter card. If the card is labeled with an *H,* have the group cheer by enthusiastically saying, "Hip, hip, hooray!" If the card is labeled with a different letter, direct youngsters to give a disappointed sigh.

Materials:
several blank cards

To get ready:
Label each card with a letter, writing *H* on most.

In the Hat
Letter recognition

Have youngsters sit in a circle. Then pass the hat to a child. Invite him to remove a manipulative from the hat and show it to the group. If the letter is an *H,* have youngsters pretend to put imaginary hats on their heads. If the letter is not an *H,* direct youngsters to do nothing. Continue passing the hat around the circle until each child has had a turn.

Materials:
class supply of letter manipulatives, mostly *H*s
hat

To get ready:
Place the manipulatives in the hat.

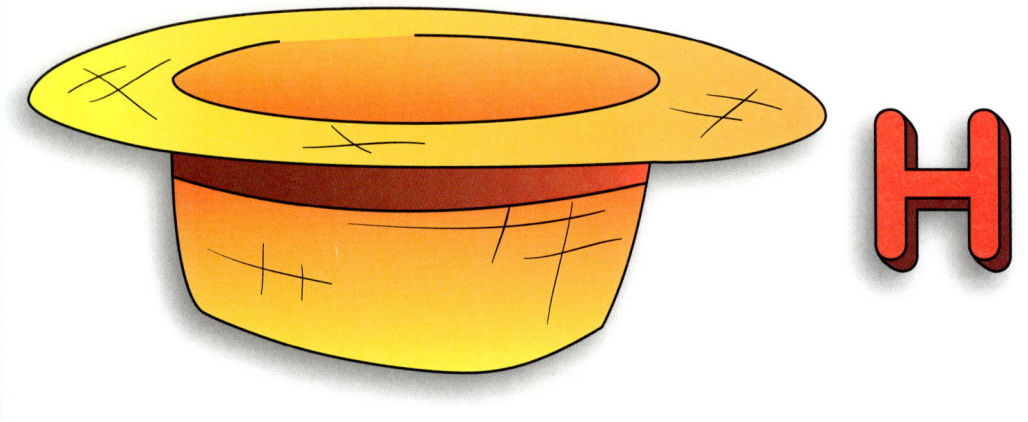

Letter Hoopla
Uppercase and lowercase letters

Invite a child to choose a card and show it to the group. Then have him place the card in the appropriate hoop. If the card is placed correctly, encourage the group to show approval with a round of applause. Continue until each child has had a turn.

Materials:
2 plastic hoops
class supply of blank cards
uppercase and lowercase *H* cutouts

To get ready:
Label each card with an uppercase or a lowercase *H*. Place the hoops and letter cutouts on the floor as shown. Stack the letter cards facedown nearby.

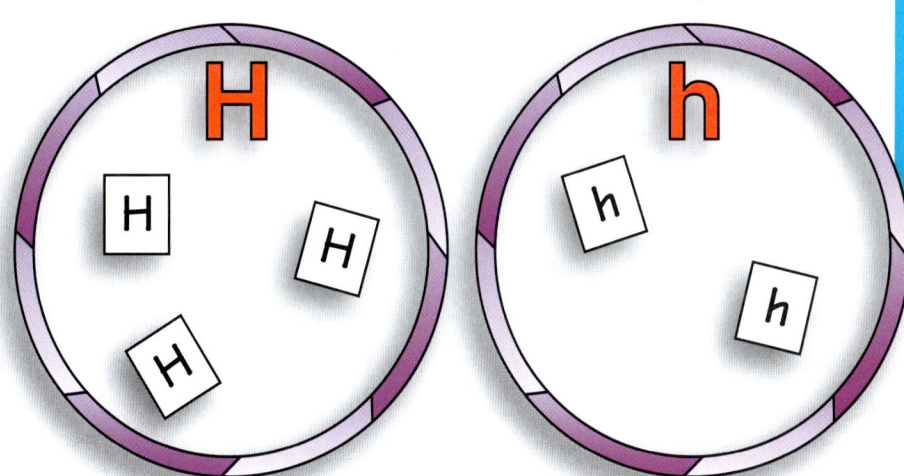

Hopping Hares
Uppercase and lowercase letters

Ask your students to pretend they are hopping hares. Then point to a letter. If the letter is an uppercase *H*, have the hares hop up high. If the letter is a lowercase *h*, direct them to hop low to the ground. Continue pointing to letters as time permits.

Materials:
pointer

To get ready:
Write several uppercase and lowercase *H*s on the board.

Island Voyage
Beginning sound /ī/

To begin, announce a word. Ask students whether the word begins with the /ī/ sound like *island*. If it does, invite a youngster to move the boat across the water to the island. If it does not, leave the boat at the water's edge. Repeat the activity, returning the boat to its original location if needed. Announce a different word and have a different child move the boat each time.

Materials:
green construction paper island cutout
boat cutout
sheet of blue construction paper (water)
glue

To get ready:
Glue the island to the water as shown; then place the boat at the opposite edge of the water.

I Is for *Igloo*
Letter-sound association

Draw a large igloo shape on the board. Invite a volunteer to take a card and show it to the group. Help youngsters read the word. Then ask the group whether the word begins with the /ĭ/ sound like *igloo*. If it does, the volunteer attaches the card inside the igloo outline. If it does not, she sets the card aside. Continue with each remaining card.

Materials:
several blank white cards
tape or Sticky-Tac adhesive

To get ready:
Label each card with a word, writing a word that begins with the /ĭ/ sound on most. Stack the cards facedown.

Ice-Cold
Letter-sound association

Give each cup to a different child. Start the music and instruct students to pass the cups around the circle. Periodically stop the music, signaling youngsters to freeze. Have the children holding the cups touch the ice inside and say, "Ice-cold ice!" Then restart the music. Repeat the activity as desired or until the ice is melted.

Materials:
supply of ice cubes
2 disposable cups
music player
music

To get ready:
Label each cup with an *I*. Then place several ice cubes in each cup.

Skating on Ice
Letter recognition

Ask students to imagine they are at an ice-skating rink. Have them demonstrate some ice-skating moves, such as skating in circles, twirling, and skating backward. After youngsters demonstrate their moves, display a card. If the card is labeled with *I*, youngsters pretend they are ice-skating. If the card is labeled with a different letter, students stand still.

Materials:
several blank cards

To get ready:
Label the cards with letters, writing *I* on most.

Dairy Delight
Letter identification

Materials:
clean, empty ice cream container
large bowl cutout
class supply of paper circles

To get ready:
Label each circle (scoop of ice cream) with a letter, writing *I* on most. Put the ice cream scoops in the container. Set the container near the bowl cutout.

Invite each child, in turn, to take a scoop of ice cream from the container and identify the letter. If the letter is *I*, the child puts the ice cream scoop above the bowl as you lead the remaining youngsters in reciting the rhyme. If the letter is not *I*, the child sets the ice cream scoop aside.

Ice cream, ice cream.
Yum, yum, yum!
Eating ice cream
Is so much fun!

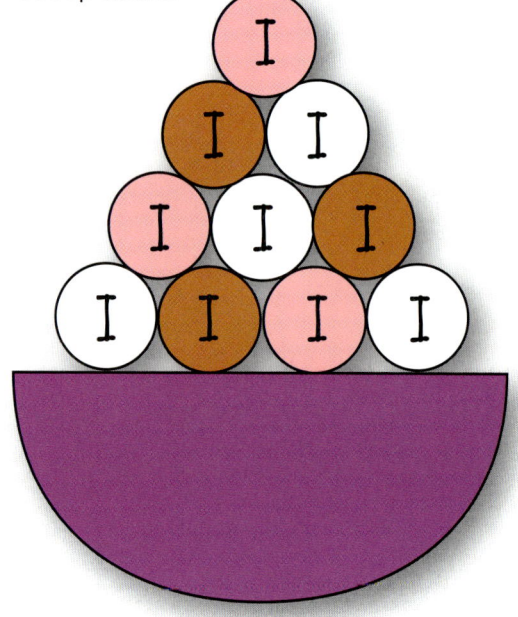

I Spy the Letter *I*
Letter identification

Materials:
large letter *I* cutout

To get ready:
No preparation is necessary.

Display the cutout and have the group identify the letter. Then instruct students to close their eyes while you hide the letter nearby. After hiding the letter, invite youngsters to open their eyes to look for it. When a child spots the letter, he calls out, "I spy the letter *I*!" Then he shows the group where the letter is. Remove the letter and repeat the activity.

I spy the letter *I*!

Which House?
Uppercase and lowercase letters

Invite each child, in turn, to take an icicle and hold it in the air. Have the group determine whether the icicle shows an uppercase or a lowercase *I*. Then ask the child to "hang" the icicle from the roof of the appropriate house. While he does so, the remaining students chant, "Icicles on the roof. Brrrr, brrrr!" as they pretend to shiver.

Materials:
class supply of white icicle-shaped cutouts
2 large house cutouts labeled as shown

To get ready:
Label each icicle cutout with either an uppercase or a lowercase *I*. Set out the houses. Put the icicles facedown nearby.

Special Sprinkles
Letter formation

Invite a volunteer to use a marker to write a letter *I* (candy sprinkle) on the ice cream as you lead the group in singing the song. Then continue with other volunteers until the ice cream is covered with letter *I* sprinkles.

Materials:
large sheet of white paper
colorful markers

To get ready:
Draw a large ice cream cone and scoop on the paper. Set the markers nearby.

(sung to the tune of "The Muffin Man")

Decorate the ice cream scoop,
The ice cream scoop, the ice cream scoop.
Decorate the ice cream scoop
With letter *I* sprinkles!

What's in the Bowl?
Beginning sound /j/

Display an object or a picture and have students say its name. Then lead youngsters in singing the song below, emphasizing each /j/ sound. Repeat the activity several times using a different object or picture each time and changing the underlined words in the song.

(sung to the tune of "The Farmer in the Dell")

[Jelly] in the bowl.	Pretend to hold a big bowl.
[Jelly] in the bowl.	
Jiggle, joggle, jiggle, joggle.	Jiggle the bowl.
[Jelly] in the bowl.	Pretend to hold a big bowl.

Materials:
objects or pictures of objects whose names begin with /j/

To get ready:
No preparation is necessary.

Happy or Sad?
Beginning sound /j/

Name a word and direct youngsters to repeat it. If the word begins like *jack-o'-lantern,* have youngsters display the happy faces of their cutouts. If the word begins differently than *jack-o'-lantern,* have them show the sad faces. Continue for several more rounds using a different word each time.

Materials:
class supply of pumpkin cutouts

To get ready:
Draw a happy jack-o'-lantern face on one side of each pumpkin and a sad jack-o'-lantern face on the other side.

Lots of Tentacles
Letter-sound association

Name a word and have students determine whether it begins with the /j/ sound. If it does, invite a volunteer to attach a tentacle to the jellyfish. Continue with different words until all the tentacles have been attached to the jellyfish.

Materials:
large jellyfish cutout
several *J* cutouts (tentacles)
Sticky-Tac adhesive

To get ready:
Post the jellyfish and set the *J*s and the adhesive nearby.

What a Treasure!
Letter-sound association

Invite a volunteer to name a word that begins with /j/. (Provide assistance if needed.) Write the word on a jewel cutout and help him tape it on the treasure chest. Continue with the remaining jewels. Then lead youngsters in saying each word, emphasizing the /j/ sound as you underline the letter.

Materials:
treasure chest cutout
colorful jewel cutouts
tape

To get ready:
Post the treasure chest, labeled as shown.

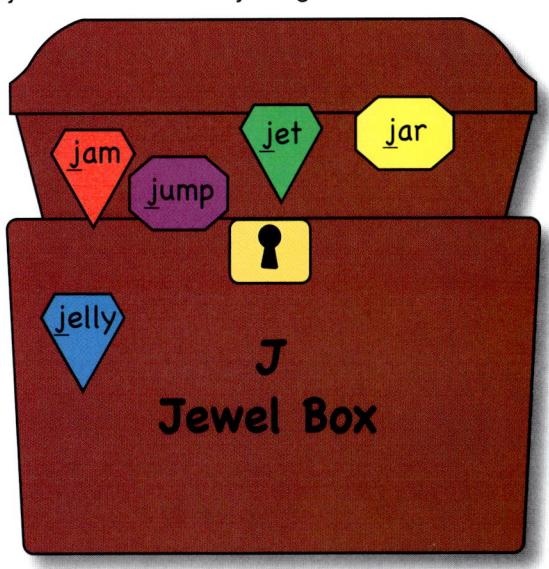

Circle Time From A to Z • ©The Mailbox® Books • TEC61276

Jelly Bean Jar
Letter recognition

Have youngsters pretend they are at a candy store to buy jelly beans labeled with *J*s. Then invite a volunteer to pick a jelly bean labeled with a *J* and place it in the bag. Continue until all the jelly beans labeled with *J* have been "purchased."

Materials:
extra-large jar cutout
several jelly bean cutouts
paper lunch bag

To get ready:
Label each jelly bean with a letter, writing *J* on most. Place the jar on the floor and arrange the jelly beans faceup on the jar. Set the bag nearby.

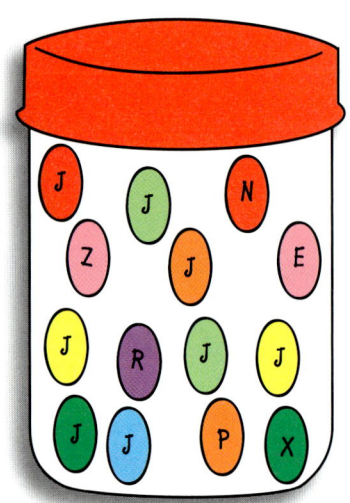
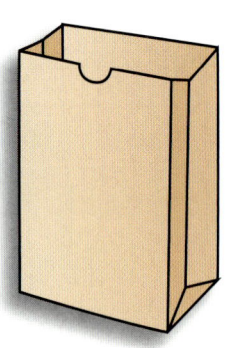

Jump for J
Letter recognition

Display a letter card. If it is labeled with a *J*, have each youngster do a jumping jack. If it is labeled with a letter other than *J*, instruct students to remain still. Continue with the remaining cards.

Materials:
several blank cards

To get ready:
Label the cards with letters, writing *J* on most.

Jiggle Like Jell-O Gelatin

Uppercase and lowercase letters

Hold up a card. If the card is labeled with an uppercase *J*, have youngsters stand up tall and jiggle their bodies like Jell-O gelatin. If the card is labeled with a lowercase *j*, instruct students to squat or sit down before jiggling their bodies. Repeat with the remaining cards.

Materials:
several blank cards

To get ready:
Label each card with an uppercase or a lowercase *J*.

Model and Make

Letter formation

On the board, model writing an uppercase *J*. Invite each group to use its jump rope and paper strip to duplicate the *J*. When the groups are finished, have students confirm that the *J*s are correct. Next, model writing a lowercase *j*, using a paper circle as the dot. Give each group a paper circle and have students make a lowercase *j* with their circle and jump rope.

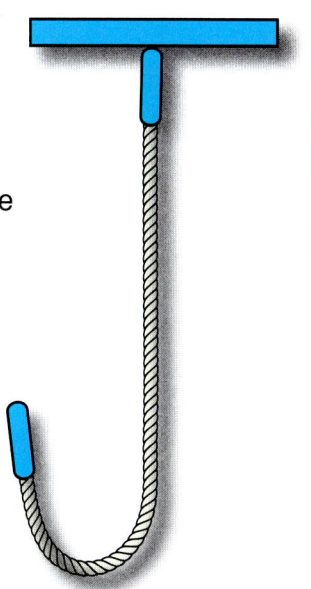

Materials:
several jump ropes
several paper strips
several paper circles

To get ready:
Arrange students in small groups and give each group a jump rope and a paper strip.

King of the K Words
Beginning sound /k/

Hand the crown to a child and start the music. Instruct students to pass the crown around the circle while the music is playing. Periodically stop the music, signaling youngsters to freeze. The child holding the crown becomes the king. Announce two words, one that begins like *king* and one that does not. The king tells which word has the beginning sound /k/. After confirming his answer, have the class repeat the word. Then restart the music. **For an added challenge,** instead of announcing the words, have the king name a word that begins with /k/.

Materials:
construction paper crown
music player
music

To get ready:
No preparation is necessary.

Can You Guess?
Beginning sound /k/

Tell students you are thinking of a word that begins with the /k/ sound. Then give one or more clues to help students guess the word. For example, for the word *key* you might say, "This object is made of metal. You use it to open a lock." Then invite a volunteer to guess the word. If she is correct, continue with other words that begin with /k/. If she is incorrect, give additional clues until a youngster determines the word.

Materials:
none

To get ready:
No preparation is necessary.

The Kangaroo Hop

Letter-sound association

Sing the song aloud. At the end of the song, hold up the sign and invite students to make the /k/ sound and hop like kangaroos.

Materials:
large letter *K* sign

To get ready:
No preparation is necessary.

(sung to the tune of "Row, Row, Row Your Boat")

K is for *kangaroo*
And makes the /k/ sound.
When you see the letter *K*,
Say /k/ and jump around!

Gentle Kick

Letter-sound association

Have students stand in a circle. Hand a child the ball and ask him to point to the letter *K*. Then have him put the ball on the floor and gently kick it to a classmate. When he kicks the ball, encourage the group to say, "*K* is for *kick!*" emphasizing each /k/ sound. The classmate who receives the ball then takes a turn. Continue until each child has had a turn kicking the ball.

Materials:
ball

To get ready:
Label the ball with a large letter *K*.

Kk Kk Kk Kk Kk Kk Kk Kk Kk Kk Kk Kk

Materials:
several blank cards

To get ready:
Label each card with a letter, writing *K* on most.

Blow a Kiss
Letter recognition

Hold a card in the air. If the card is labeled with the letter *K,* youngsters blow a kiss. If it is labeled with a different letter, youngsters remain still.

Materials:
large lock cutout
class supply of key cutouts (page 104)

To get ready:
Label each blank key with a desired letter other than the letter *K.* Set out the lock. Place the keys near the lock letter-side down.

Lock and Keys
Letter identification

Have each child turn over a key, in turn, and identify the letter shown. When the letter is *K,* the child places the key on the lock. When the letter is not *K,* she sets the key aside.

Kk Kk Kk Kk Kk Kk Kk Kk Kk

Special Delivery
Letter identification

Give the envelope to a volunteer. Lead youngsters in singing the song as the volunteer walks around the inside of the circle. When the song ends, she gives the envelope to the classmate closest to her. That child removes a card from the envelope and identifies the letter on the card. If the letter is *K*, she puts the card in the pocket chart. If it is not *K*, she sets the card aside. Then the two students switch places. The activity continues until the envelope is empty.

Materials:
several blank cards
large envelope
pocket chart

To get ready:
Label each card with a letter, writing *K* on most. Put the cards in the envelope.

(sung to the tune of "Mary Had a Little Lamb")

Delivering some letter cards,
Letter cards, letter cards.
Delivering some letter cards—
Is this one labeled *K*?

Which Kite?
Uppercase and lowercase letters

Give each child a paper strip (bow). Have her decide whether her bow shows an uppercase or a lowercase *K*. Then have her place the bow on the appropriate kite string.

Materials:
2 large kite cutouts
class supply of paper strips
yarn
tape

To get ready:
Label each paper strip with either an uppercase or a lowercase *K*. Tape a piece of yarn to the back of each kite and label the kites as shown. Place the kites on the floor.

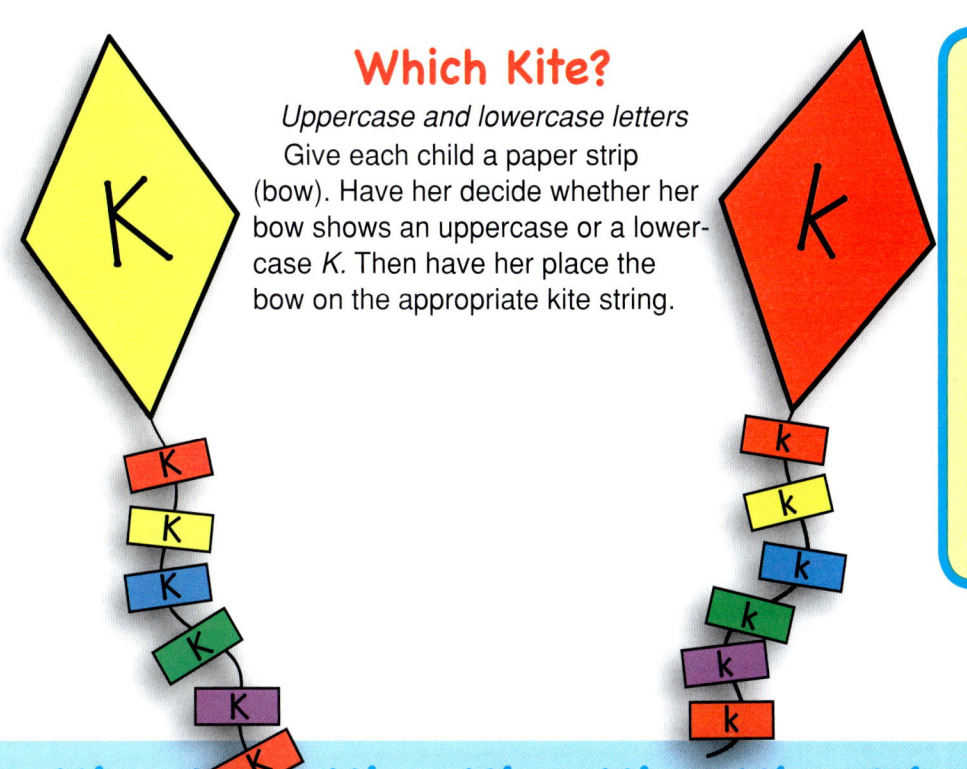

Lemons and Limes
Beginning sound /l/

On the flannelboard, arrange lemons and limes to make a pattern. Have youngsters name each fruit in the pattern, emphasizing each /l/ sound. Repeat the activity several times, inviting volunteers to use the lemons and limes to make different patterns.

Materials:
flannelboard
yellow felt lemons
green felt limes

To get ready:
No preparation is necessary.

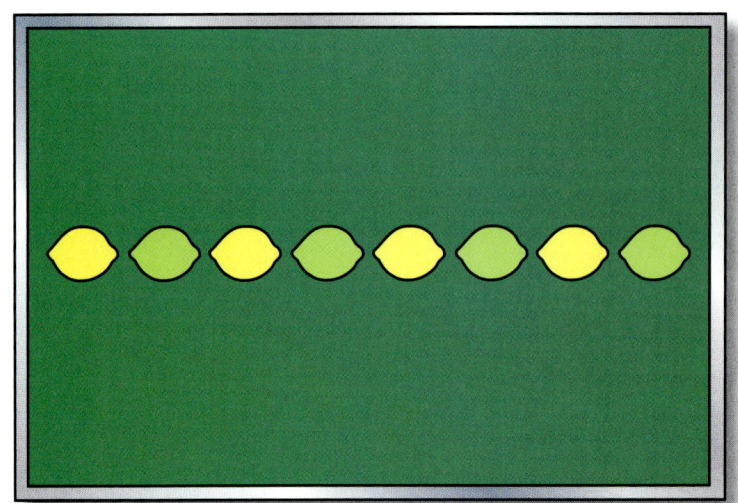

What's for Lunch?
Beginning sound /l/

Invite a volunteer to hold up a card. Have the class name the picture. If the picture's name begins like *lunch*, instruct the group to say, "Pack it!" and have the volunteer place the card in the lunchbox. If the picture's name does not begin like *lunch*, direct the group to say, "No, thanks!" and have the volunteer set the card aside. Continue in this manner with each card.

Materials:
picture cards (page 105)
lunchbox

To get ready:
Cut out a copy of the cards and stack them facedown. Set the lunchbox nearby.

On the L
Letter-sound recognition

Position the yarn on the floor to form an *L*. Ask a youngster to name the letter and encourage the class to practice making its sound. Then invite a volunteer to choose an object and show it to the class. Have the group name the object. If the name begins with the /l/ sound, have the child place the object on the *L*. If the name begins with a different sound, have him set it aside. Continue with each remaining object.

Materials:
small objects, most of whose names begin with *L* (if desired, use the picture cards on page 105)
long length of yarn

To get ready:
No preparation is necessary.

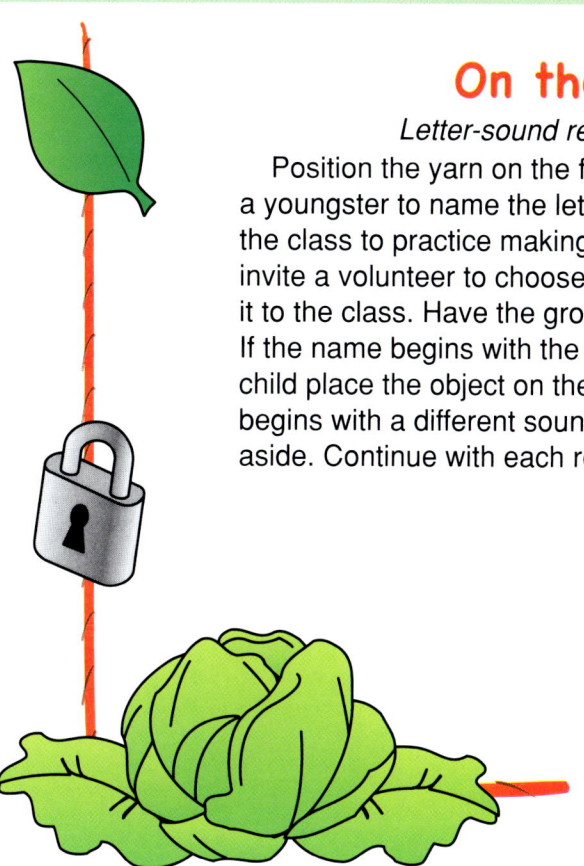

Lip-Smacking Lollipops
Letter-sound recognition

Have each child hold a lollipop. Name a word. If the word begins with the /l/ sound, have youngsters pretend to lick their lollipops. If the word does not begin with the /l/ sound, direct students to remain still. Continue for several more rounds, saying a different word each time.

Materials:
class supply of paper circles
class supply of craft sticks
tape

To get ready:
Label each circle with an *L*. To make lollipops, tape a craft stick to the back of each circle.

Lots of Leaves
Letter recognition

Gather youngsters around the tree. Invite each child to take a leaf and read the letter. If the leaf is labeled with an *L,* have him place the leaf on the tree. If not, have him place it near the base of the tree. Continue until each leaf has been placed.

Materials:
class supply of fall leaf cutouts
large tree cutout

To get ready:
Program the leaf cutouts with letters, writing *L* on most. Place the tree on the floor and set the leaves nearby.

Lion on a Ladder
Letter recognition

Invite a volunteer to display a letter card and have youngsters name the letter. If it is an *L,* lead the class in saying, "Move up, Lion," as the volunteer moves the lion up one rung. If the card is not labeled with an *L,* have them say, "Sorry, Lion," as the volunteer leaves the lion where it is. Continue in this manner until the lion reaches the top rung of the ladder.

Materials:
masking tape
toy lion or lion picture
letter cards containing mostly *L*s

To get ready:
On the floor, arrange masking tape strips to resemble a ladder. Set the letter cards (stacked facedown) and lion at the base of the ladder.

Seeing Spots
Uppercase and lowercase letters

Tell little ones that the ladybug needs help putting its spots on the correct wings. Give each child a spot. Then invite a few youngsters at a time to place their spots on the corresponding wings. After all the spots have been placed, enlist students' help in checking the placement.

Materials:
large ladybug cutout with no spots
class supply of black paper circles (spots)
white crayon

To get ready:
Use the crayon to program each spot with an uppercase or a lowercase *L*. Label the ladybug as shown and post it in a student-accessible location.

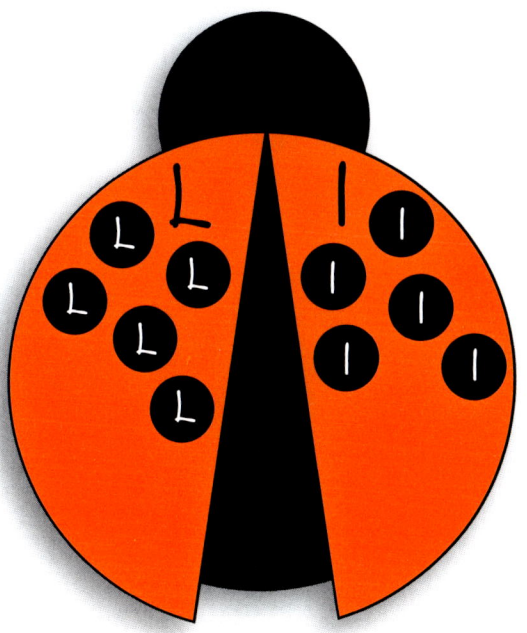

Lots of Links
Letter formation

Write a lowercase *l* on the board and have each youngster connect five links so they resemble an *l*. Then write an uppercase *L* on the board and direct each child to add the three remaining links to form an *L*.

Materials:
8 plastic links for each child

To get ready:
No preparation is necessary.

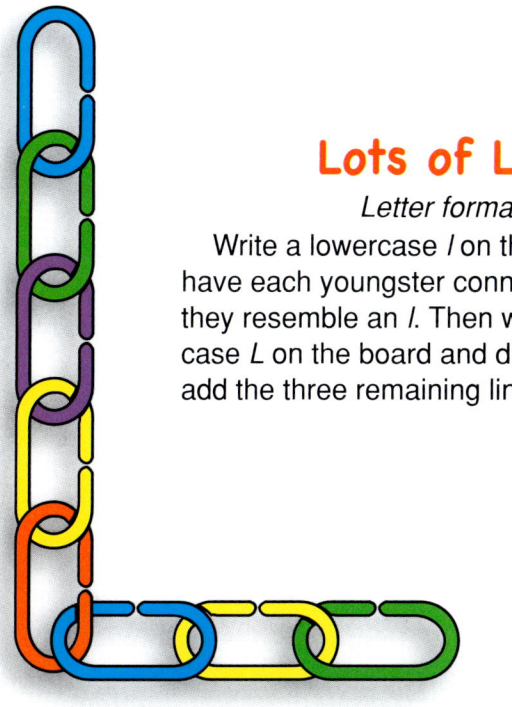

Mm

Monkey Moves
Beginning sound /m/
Review with youngsters the /m/ sound at the beginning of *monkey* and *moves.* Then say a word. If the word begins with /m/, each student moves like a monkey; if not, he remains still. After allowing enough time for your little monkeys to move, signal youngsters to stop. Continue with more words, most of which begin with /m/, as time permits.

Mustard.

Materials:
none

To get ready:
No preparation is necessary.

Materials:
classroom objects, most of whose names begin with /m/
brown yarn

To get ready:
Cut a five-foot yarn length for each child.

Mud Puddle Jump!
Beginning sound /m/
Have each youngster loop her yarn to form a circle on the floor (mud puddle). Then show and name an object. If the word begins with /m/, each child jumps inside her puddle; if it does not, she stays where she is. To continue, have each child move outside her puddle (if needed) before showing a different object.

Mug.

Circle Time From A to Z • ©The Mailbox® Books • TEC61276

Mr. Moose's Menu
Letter-sound association

Tell youngsters that Mr. Moose's menu will only include items whose names begin with /m/. Then ask youngsters, "Does Mr. Moose like [pie] or [muffins]?" Help youngsters conclude that *muffins* begins with /m/ and *pie* does not. Then guide youngsters to name the letter *m* as you write *muffins* on the menu. Continue with different word pairs (see suggestions) as time permits.

Materials: chart paper

To get ready: Label the chart paper as shown.

Word pairs: ketchup, mustard; milk, juice; mushrooms, tomatoes; chicken, meatloaf; mayonnaise, butter; mangoes, oranges; sausages, meatballs

Mirror, Mirror
Letter-sound association

Invite a child to hold the mirror and recite the chant shown. Then have him name a word that begins with *m*. Lead youngsters to conclude that the first sound in the word is /m/, so the first letter must be *m*. Write the word inside the mirror outline. Then ask the youngster to pass the mirror to a classmate to begin a new round.

Mirror, mirror, /m/, /m/, /m/.
What's a word that starts with *m*?

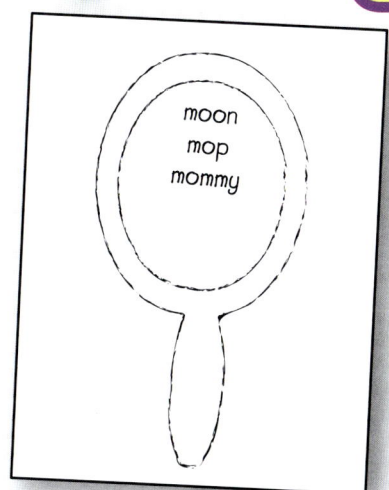

Materials: tagboard mirror cutout, chart paper

To get ready: Draw a large outline of a mirror on the paper.

Letters for Lunch
Letter recognition

Invite a youngster to pretend to be a letter monster that eats only *M*s. Next, post a strip and lead youngsters in chanting the rhyme shown. Then ask the letter monster to point to each *M* as he counts aloud. After he has pointed to each *M* (provide assistance as needed), lead youngsters in saying, "/m/, /m/, /m/." Continue with each strip, inviting a different student to be the letter monster each time. **For a more advanced version,** include uppercase and lowercase letters on the strips.

Materials:
supply of sentence strips

To get ready:
Write a different set of letters (including several *M*s) on each strip.

Letter monster,
Letter monster.
Munch, munch, munch!
How many *M*s will you eat for lunch?

Many Moons
Uppercase and lowercase letters

Give each child a moon. Then invite each child, in turn, to show her cutout to the class and identify whether it is labeled with an uppercase or a lowercase *M*. After confirming her answer, have her place her moon on the appropriate galaxy.

Materials:
class supply of crescent moon cutouts
2 large pieces of black paper (galaxies)
white crayon

To get ready:
Use the white crayon to label the sheets of paper as shown. Program each moon with either an uppercase or a lowercase *M*. Set out each galaxy.

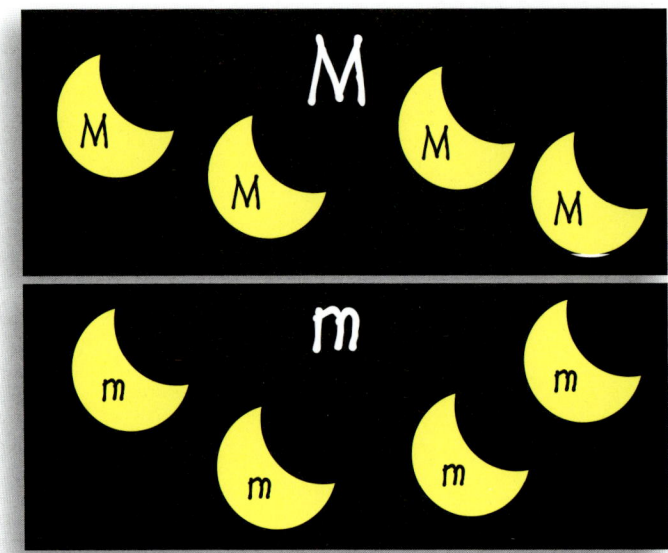

Move That Monkey!

Uppercase and lowercase letters

Tell youngsters that this silly monkey has gotten itself stuck in the mud and needs their help to get out! To begin, have a volunteer flip two cards. If he finds an uppercase and a lowercase letter pair (if desired, encourage him to seek help from classmates), he leaves the cards faceup as the group announces, "Move that monkey!" Then he moves the monkey one step closer to the grass. If it is not an uppercase and lowercase letter pair, he flips the cards back over. Continue the activity with different volunteers until the monkey is out of the mud!

Materials:
stuffed toy monkey or monkey cutout
6 papers: 5 brown (mud), 1 green (grass)
even number of blank cards (minimum of 10)
pocket chart

To get ready:
Write *M* on half the cards. Write *m* on the remaining cards. Shuffle the cards and place them facedown in the pocket chart. Place the mud and grass side by side on the floor, keeping the grass at one end. Place the monkey on the mud farthest from the grass.

Mountain-Climbing Mouse

Letter formation

Have a child use the mouse to trace the *M* on the chart while the rest of the class sings the song shown. After tracing the letter, have him write *M* in a cloud. Continue until each cloud has an *M* on it. If desired, encourage seated students to write an *M* in the air as they sing.

(sung to the tune of "The Bear Went Over the Mountain")

The mouse went over the mountain.
The mouse went over the mountain.
The mouse went over the mountain,
  to trace the letter *M*.

Materials:
stuffed toy mouse or mouse cutout
chart paper

To get ready:
On the chart paper, write a large *M* and draw several cloud shapes. Place the mouse near the chart.

Nn

In the News
Beginning sound /n/

Invite a child to choose a card and say the picture's name. If the name begins with /n/, the group says, "in the news" and the child tapes the picture to the newspaper. If the name begins with a different sound, the group says nothing and the child puts the picture aside. Continue with the remaining pictures.

Materials:
picture cards (page 106)
newspaper
tape

To get ready:
Post the newspaper and set the picture cards and tape nearby.

Touch Your Nose
Beginning sound /n/

Announce a word that begins with /n/, such as *net*. Then lead students in singing the song. Invite volunteers to name other words that begin with /n/. Repeat the song for each word, replacing *net* with the new word.

(sung to the tune of "The Farmer in the Dell")

[Net] begins with /n/.
[Net] begins with /n/.
Strike a pose and touch your nose.
[Net] begins with /n/.

Materials:
none

To get ready:
No preparation is necessary.

Put It Together
Letter-sound association

Invite a volunteer to name a word that begins with /n/. After confirming her answer, post a puzzle piece. Continue until all the pieces are posted and assembled to reveal the *N*.

Materials:
large *N* cutout
Sticky-Tac
scissors

To get ready:
Puzzle-cut the *N*.

Nice Neighbors
Letter-sound association

Point to the sign and read it aloud. Ask youngsters to imagine they live in a neighborhood where everyone has a name that begins with /n/. Then introduce the youngster next to you by saying, "This is my neighbor, [child's name]," substituting the /n/ sound for the beginning sound of the child's name. If the child's name begins with a vowel, add the /n/ sound to the beginning of his name. Have each child introduce his neighbor in this manner.

This is my neighbor, Nemily.

Materials:
sheet of paper

To get ready:
Write "The *N* Neighborhood" on the paper and then post the sign.

Make Some Noise
Letter recognition

Ask students to imagine they are fans of the Nifty *N* team. Then display a card. If the card is labeled with an *N*, youngsters make noise for the team by cheering, snapping, clapping, or stomping. If the card is labeled with a different letter, students remain quiet. Continue as described for the remaining cards.

Materials:
blank cards

To get ready:
Label the cards with letters, writing *N* on most.

In the Nest
Letter identification

Invite a volunteer to choose a letter and identify it for the group. If the letter is an *N*, the group chirps like birds and the volunteer places the letter in the nest. If the letter is not an *N*, the group remains quiet and the volunteer sets the letter aside.

Materials:
large bowl
brown paper shreds
class supply of letter manipulatives, including several *N*s

To get ready:
To make a nest, fill the bowl with paper shreds. Arrange the letters around the nest.

Noodle Soup
Uppercase and lowercase letters

Tell youngsters Chef Norman needs their help putting noodles in the correct pots. Invite a few youngsters at a time to each take a noodle and place it in the matching pot. Then remove the noodles from the pots to confirm that they were sorted correctly.

Materials:
2 pots
class supply of noodle cutouts (page 106)
blank cards
puppet (optional)

To get ready:
Label the pots as shown. Set out the pots and arrange the noodles around them. If desired, use the puppet to introduce an imaginary chef named Chef Norman.

Keeping Cool
Ending sound /n/

Review the ending sound of /n/ using a fan as a prop. Give each child a fan. Then name a word. If the word ends with /n/ like *fan*, youngsters fan themselves. If the word ends with a different sound, students hold their fans in their laps.

Pin.

Materials:
class supply of paper squares

To get ready:
Make fans by accordion-folding each square and stapling one end of the paper.

Over the Oval
Beginning sound /ō/
Have each child stand behind an oval. Call out a word. If the word begins with the /ō/ sound like *oval,* students say, "[Open] starts like *oval!*" emphasizing each /ō/ sound. Then youngsters step over their ovals. If the word begins with a different sound, students stand quietly behind their ovals.

Materials:
class supply of large ovals

To get ready:
No preparation is necessary.

Begins Like Octopus
Beginning sound /ŏ/
Give each child a copy of page 107 along with several *O*s. Announce a word. Ask the group whether the word begins with the /ŏ/ sound like *octopus.* If it does, each child attaches an *O* to one of the octopus's arms. If it does not, youngsters wait for the next word to be announced.

Materials:
class supply of page 107 hole reinforcers (letter *O*s)

To get ready:
No preparation is necessary.

Open Wide!
Letter recognition

Ask students to pretend they are at the doctor's office. Remind them how doctors sometimes use tongue depressors to check their throats. Display a craft stick (tongue depressor) and invite a volunteer to determine whether it is labeled with an *O*. If it is, youngsters say, "Open wide!" Then students open their mouths wide. If it is labeled with a different letter, youngsters keep still.

Materials:
several jumbo craft sticks

To get ready:
Label each craft stick with a letter, writing *O* on most.

Splash Your Feet
Letter recognition

Have youngsters sit in a circle. Tell them to pretend the center of the circle is the ocean. Display a card. If students determine the letter is *O*, they pretend to splash their feet in the ocean. If the letter is not *O*, youngsters stay still.

Materials:
several blank cards

To get ready:
Label each card with a letter, writing *O* on most.

O Is for Oatmeal
Letter identification

Display a card. Have students identify the letter. If the letter is *O,* youngsters chant, "*O* is for *oatmeal.* Yum, yum, yum!" as you shake the oatmeal packet. Then they pretend to eat a spoonful of oatmeal. If the letter is not *O,* students sit quietly and wait for the next card to be shown.

Materials:
packet of oatmeal
several blank cards

To get ready:
Label each card with a letter, writing *O* on most.

Orange Picking
Uppercase and lowercase letters

Invite each child, in turn, to pick an orange from the tree and hold it in the air. Have the group identify whether the letter is an uppercase or a lowercase *O.* Then ask the child to put the orange in the appropriate basket.

Materials:
class supply of orange circles
tree cutout
2 small baskets labeled as shown

To get ready:
Label the circles (oranges) with either an uppercase or a lowercase *O.* Put the oranges facedown on the tree. Set the baskets near the tree.

Hop and Bop
Letter formation

Youngsters form the letter O while singing and dancing to a familiar tune.

(sung to the tune of "The Hokey-Pokey")

Put a [tiny O] in.	Use thumb and forefinger
Put a [tiny O] out.	to form a letter O.
Put a [tiny O] in	
And then shake it all about.	
You do a hop and bop	
And then you turn yourself around.	
That's what it's all about! O, O!	

Continue with the following: *small* O (use both hands to form the letter o), *big* O (use both arms to form the letter O)

Materials:
none

To get ready:
No preparation is necessary.

Sounds Like...
Medial sound /ŏ/

Invite a child to remove a card from the box and name the picture shown. Ask the group to decide whether the name shares a sound with the word *box*. If it does *(all the cards do)*, have the child display the card in the pocket chart. Continue until all the cards are on display. Then ask students to decide what sound is in all the picture names and what letter makes the sound.

To increase the difficulty of the activity, add to the box cards that show pictures whose names do not include the short *o* sound.

Materials:
medial sounds picture cards (page 108)
small box (no lid)
pocket chart

To get ready:
Put the cards in the box.

Pepperoni Pizza, Please
Beginning sound /p/

Invite little ones to help you add pepperoni to the pizza. Have a youngster choose a pepperoni slice and name the pictured item. If the name begins like *pizza,* direct the group to say, "Put it on the pizza," emphasizing each /p/ sound. Then have the youngster attach the pepperoni slice to the pizza. If the picture begins with a different sound, have the group say, "Not on this pizza!" Then instruct the child to set the pepperoni slice aside.

Materials:
pepperoni slice cutouts (page 109)
large circle cutout
Sticky-Tac adhesive

To get ready:
Decorate the circle cutout so it looks like a cheese pizza. Post the pizza and set the pepperoni slices and adhesive nearby.

Pass the Peanuts
Beginning sound /p/

Have youngsters sit in a circle and ask them to imagine they are hungry elephants. Review the /p/ sound, using the peanuts as props, and then distribute the peanuts to several youngsters. Name a word. If the word begins like *peanut,* direct the group to say, "Please pass the peanuts," and have the youngsters holding the peanuts pass them to their neighbors. If the word begins with a different sound, direct the group to do nothing. Continue in this manner as desired.

Materials:
several peanut cutouts

To get ready:
No preparation is necessary.

Pencil.

Popping Popcorn
Letter-sound association

Ask youngsters to imagine they are popcorn kernels that are getting ready to be popped to fill the popcorn bucket. Have youngsters squat down; then name a word. If the word begins with /p/, have youngsters "pop up" as you draw a piece of popcorn in the bucket. If the word begins with a different sound, direct the youngsters to remain squatting. Continue using different words as time allows.

Materials:
none

To get ready:
On the board, draw a popcorn bucket and label it with a *P*.

Plenty of Pie
Letter-sound association

Hold the pie pan as you sit in a circle with your youngsters. Model removing an imaginary slice of pie from the pan. Pretend to eat the slice of pie as you say, "Mmmm, [pink] pie," emphasizing each /p/ sound. Pass the pan to the student beside you and invite her to imitate your actions, encouraging her to use a different /p/ word to name her pretend pie. Continue until each child has had a turn.

Materials:
disposable pie pan

To get ready:
Label the pie pan with *P*.

Mmmm, pink pie.

Pea Soup
Letter recognition

To mix up a batch of "P" soup, give each child a pea. Have each youngster, in turn, stand beside the pot. If the pea is labeled with a *P*, lead the group in saying the chant below as the child drops the pea in the pot and gives the soup a stir. If it is not, the group remains silent and the child sets the pea facedown beside the pot and then stirs the soup. Continue until each child has had a turn.

Materials:
class supply of pea cutouts
large pot
large spoon

To get ready:
Label each pea with a letter, writing *P* on most.

Put the pea in the pot.
Stir the soup until it's hot.

Popcorn in a Pan
Letter recognition

Ask youngsters to hold the edge of the tablecloth and pretend they are holding a pan. Place the popcorn cutouts in the pan. Then have students raise and lower the pan several times to "pop" the popcorn. After youngsters return the pan to the floor, invite each child to take a piece of popcorn. If the popcorn is labeled with a *P*, have the student return it to the pan. If the popcorn is labeled with a different letter, have him set it aside.

Materials:
class supply of popcorn cutouts
large round tablecloth (pan)

To get ready:
Label each cutout with a letter, writing *P* on most. Spread out the tablecloth.

Pigs on the Loose
Uppercase and lowercase letters

Tell students the pigs have gotten loose and the farmer needs help getting them back in the correct pens. Invite a youngster to take a pig and place it in the appropriate pen. If he has placed the pig in the correct pen, lead the group in saying, "Oink, oink." Continue until all the pigs are in the correct pens.

Materials:
class supply of pig cutouts (page 109)
8 brown paper strips
2 blank cards

To get ready:
Use the paper strips to make two pens like the ones shown. Label one card with *P* and the other card with *p*. Place a card above each pen and scatter the pigs around the pens.

Stop!
Ending sound /p/

Invite little ones to pretend they are police officers directing traffic. Slowly name several words. When a child hears a word that ends with /p/, have him hold out his hand to signal stop as he says, "Stop!" Repeat the process several more times, using different words each time.

Materials:
none

To get ready:
No preparation is necessary.

Quack, Quack!
Beginning sound /kw/

Invite your youngsters to pretend to be little ducks. Then announce a word. If the word begins with the /kw/ sound like *quack,* youngsters say, "Quack, quack!" as they waddle like ducks. If the word begins with a different sound, students remain still.

Materials:
none

To get ready:
No preparation is necessary.

Quick Question
Letter recognition

Hold a card in the air. If the letter on the card is *Q,* youngsters call out, "Quick question!" emphasizing each /kw/ sound. Then ask students a simple question, such as "What sound does a dog make?" Call on a volunteer to give a response to the question. If the letter on the card is not a *Q,* students sit quietly.

Materials:
several blank cards

To get ready:
Label each card with a letter, writing *Q* on most.

Qs for the Queen
Letter identification

Pretend you are a queen. Hold a card in the air and have students identify the letter. If the letter is *Q*, youngsters say, "*Q* is for *queen!*" and then curtsy or bow to the queen. If the letter is not *Q*, youngsters remain silent and stand still.

Materials:
several blank cards

To get ready:
Label each card with a letter, writing *Q* on most.

Flipping Over Q
Uppercase and lowercase letters

Give each child a quarter. On your signal, have youngsters flip their quarters onto the floor. Then, in turn, have each child show to the group the side of her quarter that landed faceup and identify the letter. Make a tally mark on the board for each uppercase and lowercase *Q* as shown. Then lead students in counting the tally marks for each letter and comparing the results.

Materials:
class supply of gray tagboard circles (quarters)

To get ready:
Label one side of each quarter with an uppercase *Q* and the other side with a lowercase *q*. Write an uppercase *Q* and a lowercase *q* on the board.

Circle Time From A to Z • ©The Mailbox® Books • TEC61276

Rowing and Rocking
Beginning sound /r/

Have each pair of youngsters sit facing each other in an imaginary boat. Tell them to pretend to row their boats down a river. Then lead them in singing and performing the song. Emphasize each /r/ sound throughout the performance. Then lead students in repeating the song, substituting the word *rock* and performing the corresponding action.

Materials:
none

To get ready:
No preparation is necessary.

(sung to the tune of
"Row, Row, Row Your Boat")

[Row], [row], [row] your boat
Gently down the river.
Carefully, carefully, carefully, carefully—
If you fall, you'll shiver.

R-r-r-rabbit!
Beginning sound /r/

Have a youngster close her eyes while another child hides the rabbit. Then direct the child to open her eyes and search for the rabbit. As she searches, encourage her classmates to repeat the /r/ sound, saying it quietly when the child is far away from the rabbit and increasing in volume as she moves closer. Congratulate the child when she finds the rabbit. Then play another round with new volunteers.

Materials:
stuffed toy rabbit or rabbit cutout

To get ready:
No preparation is needed.

Working on the Railroad

Letter-sound association

Ask youngsters to imagine that a railroad company needs their help building a railroad. Give a volunteer a track and then announce two words—one beginning with *R*. Direct the youngster to name the word that begins with *R* like *railroad* and then have him lay the first track. Continue in this manner until all the tracks have been laid. After taping down the tracks, line up youngsters to create a train and then "chug" across the railroad tracks.

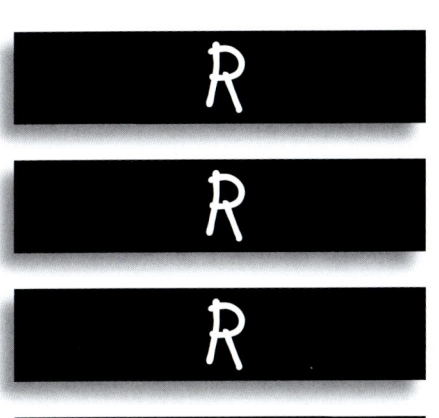

Materials:
class supply of black tagboard strips (railroad tracks)
white crayon
tape

To get ready:
Use the white crayon to program each railroad track with the letter *R*.

In the Box

Letter-sound association

Point to the *R* on the box and have the group make the /r/ sound. Tell students that there are several things in the box that begin with /r/. Give clues to describe one of the pictures until a volunteer correctly names the picture. After the picture has been identified, remove it from the box and show it to the class. Continue in the same manner with the remaining pictures.

Materials:
pictures of objects whose names begin with *R*
box with a lid

To get ready:
Label the box with an *R*. Place the pictures in the box.

Rain on the Roses
Letter recognition

Materials:
class supply of rose cards (page 110)
music
music player

To get ready:
Program each rose with a letter, using mostly *R*s. Tape the cards in a large circle on the floor.

Have students imagine they are raindrops that must water a garden of roses. Direct them to walk around the outside of the circle as you play a lively music selection. Stop the music and have each child stand behind the closest rose. If the letter *R* is on her rose, she pretends to be a raindrop and "waters" the rose by wiggling her fingers over it. If the letter is not an *R,* she stands still. After checking for accuracy, begin the music again and repeat the activity.

Lots of Robots
Letter recognition

Materials:
large blank cards

To get ready:
Label the cards with letters, writing *R* on most.

Model for youngsters how a robot moves. Then display a card. If the card is labeled with an *R,* have each child move like a robot. If the card is labeled with a different letter, direct each youngster to stand still. Continue with the remaining cards.

Rah, Rah, R!
Letter identification

Give each youngster several streamers and model how to hold the streamers to make a pom-pom. Then display a letter card. If the letter is an *R*, have each child shake his pom-pom as he says, "Rah, rah, *R!*" If it is a different letter, direct each child to remain still. Continue with each card.

Materials:
several red crepe paper streamers for each child
blank cards

To get ready:
Label each card with a letter, writing *R* on most.

It's Raining, It's Pouring
Uppercase and lowercase letters

Give each child a raindrop. Then invite a few youngsters at a time to place their raindrops under the matching clouds as the rest of the group recites the rhyme. Continue until all the raindrops have been placed.

Little raindrops
Fall from clouds
Gently, gently,
To the ground.

Materials:
2 large cloud cutouts
class supply of raindrop cutouts

To get ready:
Label the clouds as shown. Then label each raindrop with an uppercase or a lowercase *R.* Set out the clouds.

Circle Time From A to Z • ©The Mailbox® Books • TEC61276

Ss

All Packed
Beginning sound /s/

Invite a volunteer to take a card and name the picture shown. Ask the group to determine whether the picture's name begins like *suitcase.* If it does, the child puts the card in the suitcase. If it does not, he sets the card aside. Continue until all the appropriate cards are in the suitcase. To conclude the activity, remove each card, in turn, and lead youngsters in naming each item, emphasizing its beginning sound.

Materials:
picture cards (page 111)
small suitcase (or suitcase cutout)

To get ready:
Open the suitcase (or set out the cutout). Stack the cards nearby.

Tongue Twister Fun
Beginning sound /s/

Invite youngsters to practice the beginning sound /s/ while saying these giggle-inducing tongue twisters! Copy one or more tongue twisters on chart paper. Then lead students in reciting a tongue twister, emphasizing each /s/ sound. Continue with different tongue twisters as desired.

Materials:
none

To get ready:
No preparation is necessary.

Suggested tongue twisters:
Susie silently sipped salty soup.
Sandy saw seven seals at the seashore.
Seth sat in the sun singing silly songs.
Six socks sit in a sink, soaking in soap suds.
Sal and Sara saw Sam sitting sideways in the sandbox.

Susie silently sipped salty soup!

Circle Time From A to Z • ©The Mailbox® Books • TEC61276

Time to Wash
Letter-sound association

Give each child a bar of soap. Announce a word. If the word begins with /s/, youngsters pretend to use their soap to wash their bodies. If the word begins with a different sound, youngsters keep still.

Materials: class supply of construction paper rectangles (bars of soap)

To get ready: Label each rectangle with an *S*.

Letter S Soup
Letter-sound association

Give each youngster a letter *S* cutout. Call out two words: one that begins with /s/ and one that does not. Ask a child which word begins with /s/. After the child names the correct word, he places his letter *S* on the bowl as the class says, "Yum, yum, *S* soup," and youngsters rub their tummies. Continue in this way until each child has added his letter *S* to the soup.

Materials: large soup bowl cutout class supply of letter *S* cutouts

To get ready: Set out the soup bowl cutout.

Silly Sally
Letter recognition

Materials: several blank cards

To get ready: Label each card with a letter, writing *S* on most.

Have students stand. Hold a card in the air. If the card is labeled with *S*, youngsters call out, "Silly Sally says sit!" and then quickly sit on the floor. Students then return to a standing position before the next card is shown. If the card is labeled with a different letter, youngsters remain standing.

Super Sand Castle
Letter identification

Materials: class supply of light brown paper squares and rectangles; plastic pail

To get ready: Label each shape with a letter, writing *S* on most. Put the shapes in the pail.

Give the pail to a child. Instruct students to pass the pail around the circle as you lead the group in chanting, "*S* is for *summer* and *super sand castles!*" At the end of the chant, have the child holding the pail remove a shape and identify the letter. If the letter is *S*, the child puts the shape in the center of the circle to begin making a sand castle. If the letter is not *S*, she sets the shape aside. Continue in this manner until each child has had a turn.

Sizzling Sun Rays
Letter identification

Have each child, in turn, turn over a ray and identify the letter. If the letter is *S,* youngsters call out, "*S* is for *sun!*" Then the child places the ray near the edge of the sun. If the letter is not *S,* the child sets the ray aside.

Materials:
large yellow circle (sun)
class supply of yellow triangles (rays)

To get ready:
Label each ray with a letter, writing *S* on most. Set out the sun. Place the rays facedown nearby.

Sorting Socks
Uppercase and lowercase letters

Invite each child, in turn, to pick a sock and show the letter to his classmates. Have the group determine whether the letter is an uppercase or a lowercase *S.* Then have the child put the sock in the appropriate basket.

Materials:
class supply of sock cutouts
2 small baskets

To get ready:
Label each sock with either an uppercase *S* or a lowercase *s.* Set out the baskets labeled as shown. Put the socks facedown nearby.

Tt

Camping Out
Beginning sound /t/

Review the /t/ sound using the tent as a prop. Then have a volunteer choose an object and say its name as he shows it to the group. If the object's name begins with /t/ like *tent,* direct the group members to each give a thumbs-up. Then have the volunteer place the object in the tent. If the object's name begins with a different sound, have the group members each give a thumbs-down and direct the student to set the object aside.

Materials:
tagboard rectangle
small objects or pictures of objects, most of whose names begin with /t/

To get ready:
Make a tent by folding the tagboard in half as shown. Set out the tent and place the objects or pictures nearby.

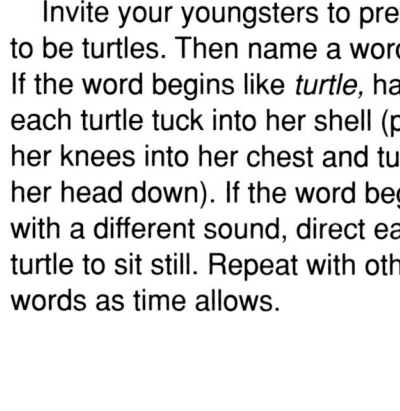

Turtle Tuck
Beginning sound /t/

Invite your youngsters to pretend to be turtles. Then name a word. If the word begins like *turtle,* have each turtle tuck into her shell (pull her knees into her chest and tuck her head down). If the word begins with a different sound, direct each turtle to sit still. Repeat with other words as time allows.

Materials:
none

To get ready:
No preparation is necessary.

Timmy the Tiger
Letter-sound association

Read the sentence starter to the group. Invite a volunteer to choose a picture and place it at the end of the sentence. Then have him lead the class in reading the sentence, emphasizing each /t/ sound. Continue with the remaining pictures. Guide students to notice all the things that Timmy eats begin with *T,* just like his name.

Materials:
pictures whose names begin with *t*
sentence strip
pocket chart

To get ready:
Program the sentence strip as shown. Place the sentence strip and pictures in a pocket chart.

Three in a Row
Letter-sound association

Divide the class into two groups and assign each group a different-colored marker. In turn, have a child from each group come to the board. Ask the student to name a word that begins with /t/. (Encourage him to ask a teammate for assistance if needed.) After he names the word, have him write a *T* on the grid where desired. Play continues until one group gets three of its *T*s in a row, or until all the spaces are filled.

Materials:
none

To get ready:
Draw a tic-tac-toe grid on the board.

Toe Touches
Letter recognition

Display a letter card. If it is labeled with a *T,* have youngsters bend down and touch their toes. If it is labeled with a different letter, instruct students to remain still. Continue with the remaining cards.

Materials:
several blank cards

To get ready:
Label each card with a letter, writing *T* on most.

A Toothy Grin
Letter identification

Give each youngster a tooth. In turn, have each child hold his tooth in the air and have the class identify the letter. If his tooth is labeled with a *T,* direct him to place the tooth in the mouth. If his tooth is labeled with a different letter, have him set it aside.

Materials:
class supply of blank cards (teeth)
extra large open mouth cutout with no teeth

To get ready:
Label each tooth with a letter, writing *T* on most. Set out the mouth.

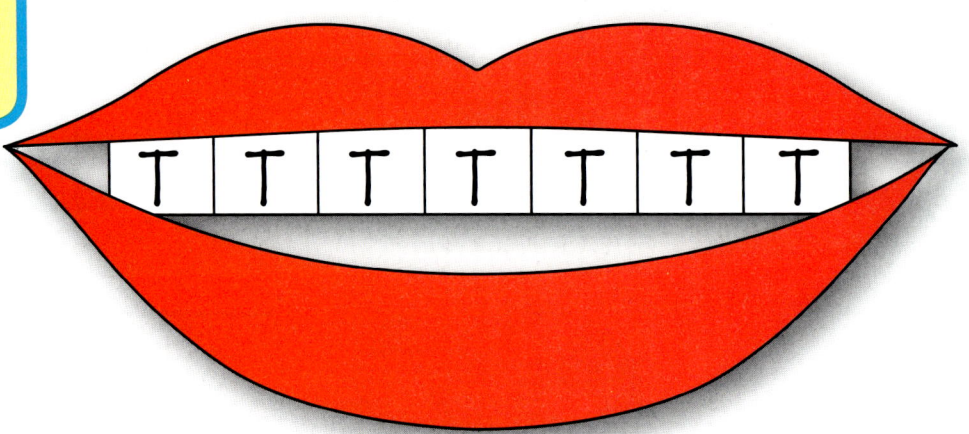

Tall Towers
Uppercase and lowercase letters

Tell youngsters they are going to build an uppercase *T* tower and a lowercase *t* tower. Then give each child a sticky note and invite students to predict which tower will be taller. Have each child, in turn, place her sticky note above the matching letter. Then lead students in counting the number of sticky notes in each tower to check their predictions.

Materials: class supply of sticky notes

To get ready: Program each sticky note with *T* or *t*, varying the number of sticky notes labeled with each case. Label the board as shown.

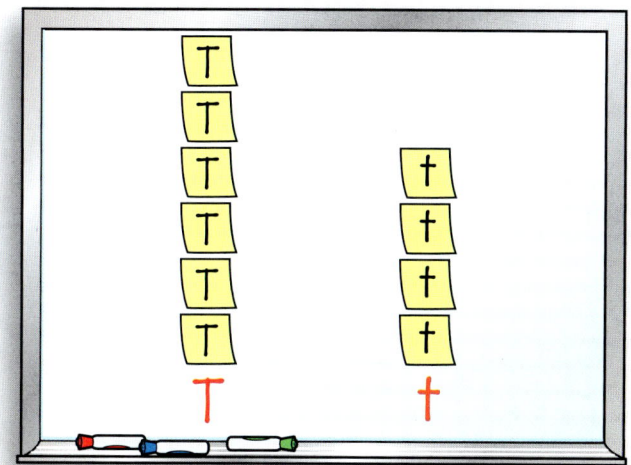

What a Catch!
Ending sound /t/

Review the ending sound /t/ using the net as a prop. Tell youngsters to pretend they are each holding a net that can only hold objects whose names end with /t/ like *net*. Name an object and then pretend to toss it in the air. If the object's name ends with /t/, have each child pantomime catching it in her net. If it ends with a different sound, have youngsters shake their heads as they say, "Not in this net." Continue naming objects as time permits.

Materials: net

To get ready: No preparation is necessary.

Looking for U!

Beginning sound /ū/

Help a student secretly hide the *U*-shaped cutout in a place that can be seen from the circle-time area. On your signal, have the other students look for the cutout as they chant "U, U, where are you?" emphasizing each long *u* sound. After the cutout has been found, invite a different youngster to hide the cutout to play another round.

Materials:
U-shaped cutout

To get ready:
No preparation is necessary.

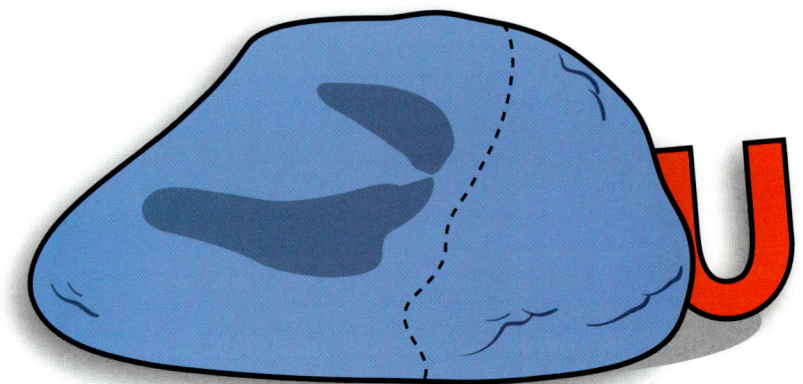

Under the Umbrella

Beginning sound /ŭ/

Invite a child to hold the umbrella above her head. Have her classmates pat the floor to make rain sounds as they recite the rhyme below, emphasizing the /ŭ/ sounds. At the end of the rhyme, direct the child who has the umbrella to pass it to a friend. Continue until each child has had a turn holding the umbrella.

Materials:
umbrella cutout

To get ready:
No preparation is necessary.

Under the umbrella, who do we see?
We see [child's name] as dry as can be.
Uh-uh-oh! The umbrella's caught in the wind.
Where will the umbrella's journey end?

Hold 'em High
Letter-sound association

Invite each child to sit holding her *U* in her lap. Name a word. If the word begins with the long *u* sound, direct the child to hold her *U* above her head. If the word begins with a different sound, have her keep her *U* in her lap. Continue with other words as time allows.

Materials:
class supply of *U* cutouts

To get ready:
No preparation is necessary.

Unicorn Horns
Letter recognition

Give each youngster a unicorn horn. Hold up a letter card and ask a volunteer to name the letter. If the letter is a *U,* have each child hold his horn to his forehead. If it is a different letter, direct him to sit quietly.

Materials:
class supply of paper cones (unicorn horns)
set of letter cards containing several *U*s

To get ready:
No preparation is necessary.

Van Drivers
Beginning sound /v/

Ask youngsters to pretend they are driving vans. Then name a word. If the word begins with /v/ like *van,* have youngsters continue driving along. If the word begins with a different sound, ask them to pretend to put on the brakes to stop their vans. To repeat the activity, have students continue driving or begin driving again as you name a different word.

Materials:
none

To get ready:
No preparation is necessary.

Make a V
Letter-sound association

To begin, show youngsters how to use two craft sticks to make a *V*. Then name a word. If the word begins with /v/, have each student use her craft sticks to form a *V* and hold it up. If the word begins with a different sound, direct each child to keep her sticks in her lap.

Materials:
2 craft sticks for each child

To get ready:
No preparation is necessary.

On the Vine
Letter identification

Give a letter to each child. Invite a few students at a time to stand in front of the group. Have each child, in turn, identify his letter. If his letter is a *V,* have the child use Sticky-Tac to attach his letter to a vine. If it is not, have him set the letter aside.

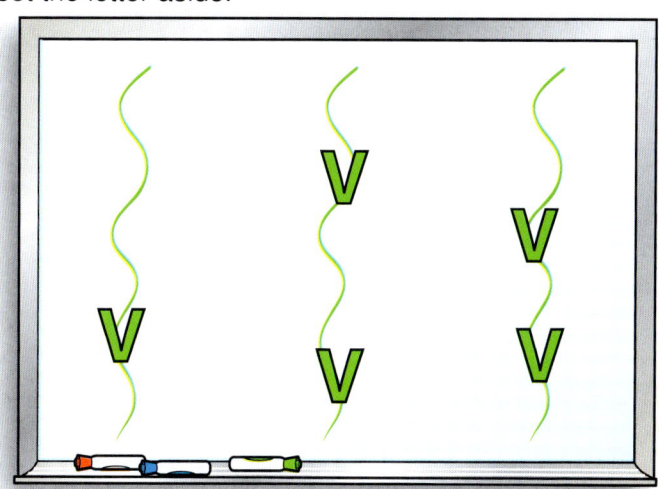

Materials:
class supply of letter cutouts, most of which are *V*s
Sticky-Tac adhesive

To get ready:
Draw several vines on the board.

Vases of Vs
Uppercase and lowercase letters

Give each youngster a flower. Invite each child, in turn, to put her flower by the correct vase. Continue until each child has put her flower by a vase. Then enlist students' help in verifying that the flowers are by the appropriate vases.

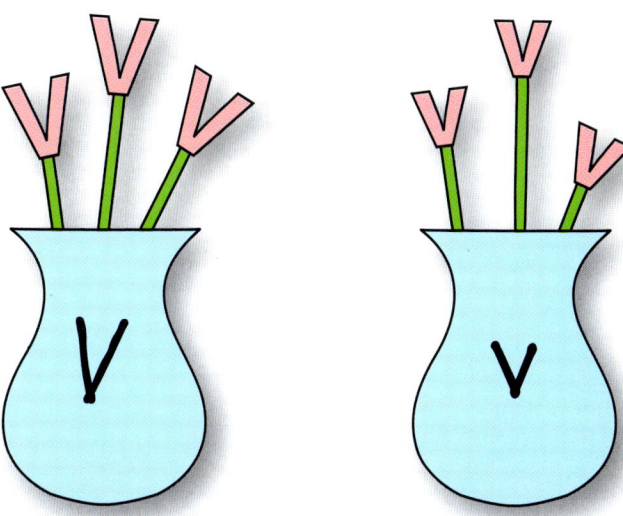

Materials:
2 large vase cutouts
a *V* or *v* cutout for each child
class supply of green paper strips (stems)

To get ready:
To make flowers, glue a letter to each stem. Label the vases as shown and then set them out.

Ww

Wiggly Worms
Beginning sound /w/

Give each child a worm. Display a card and have students name the picture shown. If it begins with /w/, youngsters wiggle their worms and say, "Wiggle on your way, little worm!" emphasizing each /w/ sound. If the name begins with a different sound, students keep their worms still.

Wiggle on your way, little worm!

Materials:
beginning sound cards (page 112)
class supply of rubber bands

To get ready:
Cut out the cards. Cut each rubber band (worms).

Weave a Web
Beginning sound /w/

Have students sit in a circle, and hand the ball of yarn to a child. Announce two words, one of which begins with /w/. Ask the child to tell which word begins like *web*. After confirming her answer, instruct her to hold the loose end of the yarn with one hand while she rolls the ball of yarn to a classmate using her other hand. Repeat the activity with different students to create a web.

Materials:
ball of yarn

To get ready:
No preparation is necessary.

Guessing W Words

Letter-sound association

Help students identify the letters on the paper and lead them in saying the /w/ sound. Then tell youngsters you are thinking of a word that begins with /w/. Give students one or more clues to help them guess the word. When a child guesses the word, write it on the paper, directing students' attention to the *w* in the word as you write it. Then lead youngsters in saying the word, emphasizing the /w/ sound.

Materials:
large sheet of paper

To get ready:
Label the top of the paper as shown.

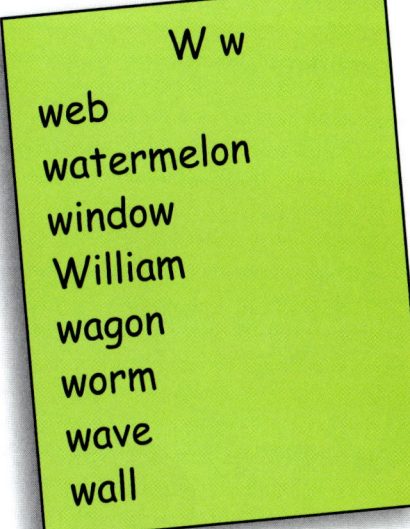

W w
web
watermelon
window
William
wagon
worm
wave
wall

Wave Your Wand

Letter recognition

Display a letter card. If the letter on the card is *W,* students wave their wands in the air while singing the song. If the letter is not *W,* youngsters hold their wands still.

(sung to the chorus of "Jingle Bells")

Wave your wand, wave your wand,
Wave it way up high.
When you see a *W,*
Wave your wand up high!

Materials:
several blank cards
class supply of craft sticks (wands)

To get ready:
Label each card with a letter, writing *W* on most.

Watermelon Seeds
Letter recognition

Invite each child, in turn, to turn over a seed. If the seed is labeled with *W*, the child leaves it faceup on the watermelon slice. If the seed is labeled with a different letter, he removes it from the watermelon slice and sets it aside.

Materials:
large watermelon slice cutout
class supply of seed cutouts

To get ready:
Label each seed cutout with a letter, writing *W* on most. Put the seeds facedown on the watermelon slice.

W Is for Wall
Letter identification

Invite a youngster to wear the hat or tool belt. Ask her to choose a block; then have the group identify the letter. If the block is labeled with *W,* she places it on the floor to begin building a wall. If the block is labeled with a different letter, she sets it aside. Continue in the same way, instructing students to stack the blocks labeled with *W* to form a wall.

Materials:
class supply of rectangular blocks
plastic construction worker hat or child's tool belt (optional)
masking tape

To get ready:
Attach a piece of tape to each block. Label each piece of tape with a letter, writing *W* on most.

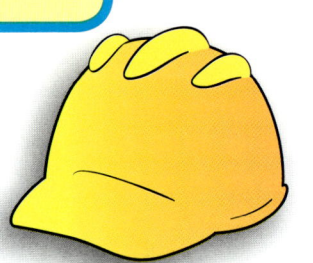
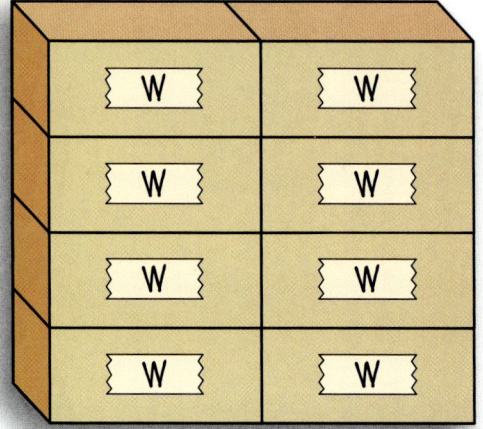

Pass the Wallet
Uppercase and lowercase letters

Hand the wallet to a child and start the music. Instruct youngsters to pass the wallet around the circle. Periodically stop the music, signaling students to freeze. The child holding the wallet removes a square, identifies the letter as an uppercase or a lowercase *W,* and then puts the square in the appropriate pile. Restart the music and continue until each child has removed a square from the wallet.

Materials:
wallet
class supply of paper squares (sized to fit the wallet)
music player
music

To get ready:
Label each paper square with either an uppercase *W* or a lowercase *w.* Store the squares in the wallet.

Ride the Wave
Letter formation

Give each student an ocean and a walrus card. Have him place the card in the ocean as shown. Then call out, "Walrus rides the wave!" Have each child move his card along the *W,* pretending his walrus is riding the wave. Repeat the activity several times.

Materials:
class supply of the beginning sound walrus card (page 112)
class supply of blue construction paper

To get ready:
Label each sheet of paper (ocean) with a large *W* (wave).

Marching for Xs
Letter recognition

Start the music and have students march inside the circle of chairs. Periodically stop the music, signaling each child to sit in the nearest chair and pick up the card. If his card is labeled with an *X*, the child holds it in the air. If the card is not labeled with an *X*, he holds it in his lap. After confirming the students' choices, instruct youngsters to return the cards beneath their chairs. Then restart the music!

Materials:
large letter *X* sign
class supply of blank cards
class supply of chairs
music player
music

To get ready:
Label each card with a letter, writing *X* on several. Arrange the chairs in a circle, facing toward the center of the circle. Place a card beneath each chair. Post the sign.

Is It an *X*?
Letter recognition

Place a card facedown on the floor in front of each student. Have each child, in turn, turn over her card. When the letter is an *X*, youngsters cross their forearms to form the letter *X*. When it is a different letter, youngsters keep still.

For a more active version, have youngsters stand in an open space with their hands on their hips. Hold a card in the air. When the letter is an *X*, students do a jumping jack to make a full body *X*. When the letter is not an *X*, youngsters keep their hands on their hips.

Materials:
class supply of blank cards

To get ready:
Label each card with a letter, writing *X* on most.

Lift and Look
Letter identification

Invite a volunteer to lift a sticky note to show the hidden letter. If the letter is an *X,* youngsters call out, "*X* marks the spot!" and the volunteer removes the sticky note and hands it to you. If the letter is not an *X,* students call out, "Too bad, so sad," and the volunteer leaves the sticky note in place. (Mark the note to remind youngsters that the letter has been viewed.) Continue with other volunteers until each *X* is uncovered.

Materials:
large sheet of paper
sticky notes

To get ready:
Label the paper with letters, writing several *X*s. Conceal each letter with a sticky note. Post the paper.

Tap, Tap, X!
Letter formation

Instruct each child to tap his sticks together when you say "tap" and to use his sticks to make the letter *X* when you say "*X*." Then announce varying sequences of *tap* and *X,* such as the following: Tap, tap, tap, tap, *X.* Tap, tap, *X.* Tap, tap, tap, *X.* Tap, *X.*

Materials:
large letter *X* sign
2 jumbo craft sticks for each child

To get ready:
Post the sign.

Yy

The Name Game
Beginning sound /y/

Display the ball of yarn and have youngsters say its name and its beginning sound. Then give the yarn to a child. Lead the group in reciting the chant, replacing the beginning sound of the child's name with /y/. If the child's name begins with a vowel, add /y/ to the beginning of her name. At the end of the chant, have the child roll the ball of yarn to a classmate. Repeat the activity until each child has had a turn.

Materials:
ball of yarn

To get ready:
No preparation is necessary.

Let's say your name
In a different way.
Instead of [Jody],
Let's say [Yody]!

Sing for Y
Letter-sound association

Invite two volunteers to each pick a card. Help each student read the word on his card. Then have each youngster place his card in the pocket chart in one of the spaces provided. Lead the group in singing the words on the sentence strips to the tune of "Frère Jacques." At the end of the song, remove the cards and set them aside. Repeat the activity with the remaining cards.

Materials:
pocket chart
4 sentence strips
even number of blank cards

To get ready:
Label each card with a word that begins with /y/. Program the sentence strips as shown, leaving two spaces in the third strip for the cards. Put the strips in the chart as shown. Place the cards nearby.

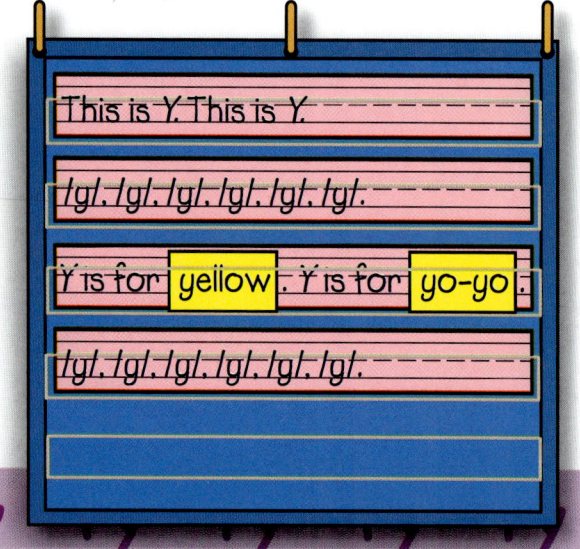

This is Y. This is Y.
/y/. /y/. /y/. /y/. /y/. /y/.
Y is for yellow. Y is for yo-yo.
/y/. /y/. /y/. /y/. /y/. /y/.

Y Is for Yawn
Letter recognition

Display a card. If it is labeled with *Y,* students say, "*Y* is for *yawn,*" and then slowly stretch as they act out an exaggerated yawn. If the letter is not *Y,* students stay still.

Y is for yawn.

Materials:
several blank cards

To get ready:
Label each card with a letter, writing *Y* on most.

Is It a Y?
Letter identification

Display a card and have students identify the letter. If the letter is *Y,* each child stands with her feet together and stretches her arms out beside her head to make a *Y* with her body. If the letter is not *Y,* each youngster stands still.

Materials:
several blank cards

To get ready:
Label each card with a letter, writing *Y* on most.

Zebra Stripes
Letter-sound association

Name a word. If the word begins with /z/, students nod their heads to signal yes. Then invite a volunteer to draw a line that zigzags so it resembles a zebra stripe on the cutout. If the word begins with a different sound, students shake their heads to signal no.

Materials:
extra large *Z* cutout
black marker

To get ready:
Post the cutout in a student-accessible location and set the marker nearby.

Loose at the Zoo
Letter identification

Tell youngsters that the letters at the zoo have gotten loose and they are zookeepers who need to return the *Z*s to the cage. Invite a few volunteer zookeepers to each find a *Z* and place it on the cage. Continue until each child has had a turn. To conclude, invite the zookeepers to confirm that each *Z* is on the cage and that there are no other letters on the cage.

Materials:
large cage cutout
class supply of *Z* cutouts plus a few additional letter cutouts

To get ready:
Place the cage on the floor and arrange the letters around it.

Catching Some Zs
Letter recognition

To begin, explain to youngsters that "to catch some Zs" means to sleep. Then hold up a letter card. If the card is labeled with a Z, each child pretends he is asleep. If the card is labeled with a different letter, the child stays awake. If youngsters are pretending to sleep, "wake" the group before displaying the next card. Continue as described for the remaining cards.

Materials:
several blank cards

To get ready:
Label the cards with letters, writing Z on most.

Buzzing Bees
Ending sound /z/

Ask little ones to pretend they are bees that are listening for /z/ at the end of words. Then name a word. If the word ends with /z/ like *buzz*, youngsters buzz like bees, emphasizing the /z/ sound. If the word ends with a different sound, the bees remain silent.

Materials:
none

To get ready:
No preparation is necessary.

Aa Medial /ă/ Picture Cards
Use with "A Stylish Hat" on page 7.

Cookie Patterns Cc
Use with "Tray of Cookies" on page 12.

Circle Time From A to Z • ©The Mailbox® Books • TEC61276

Dd **Duck Patterns**
Use with "Where Is *D*?" on page 17 and "Darling Ducks" on page 19.

Dd **Dinosaur Pattern**
Use with "Dots for Dinosaur" on page 18.

Eagle Pattern
Use with *"E Like Eagle"* on page 20.

Ee

Elf Pattern
Use with *"Elf Helpers"* on page 23.

Ee

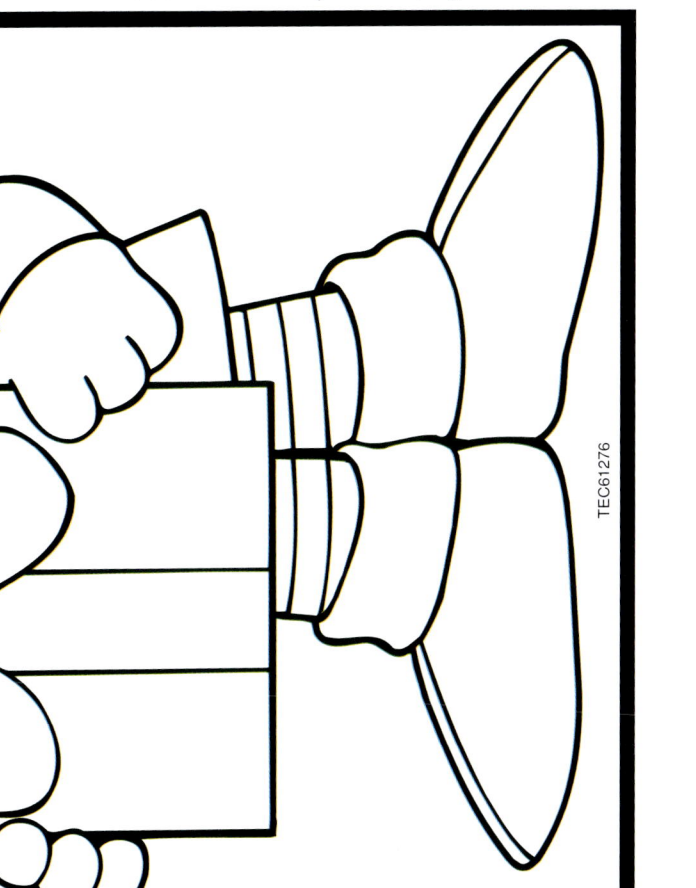

Circle Time From A to Z • ©The Mailbox® Books • TEC61276

Ff **Firefly Cards**
Use with "Fluttering Fireflies" on page 27.

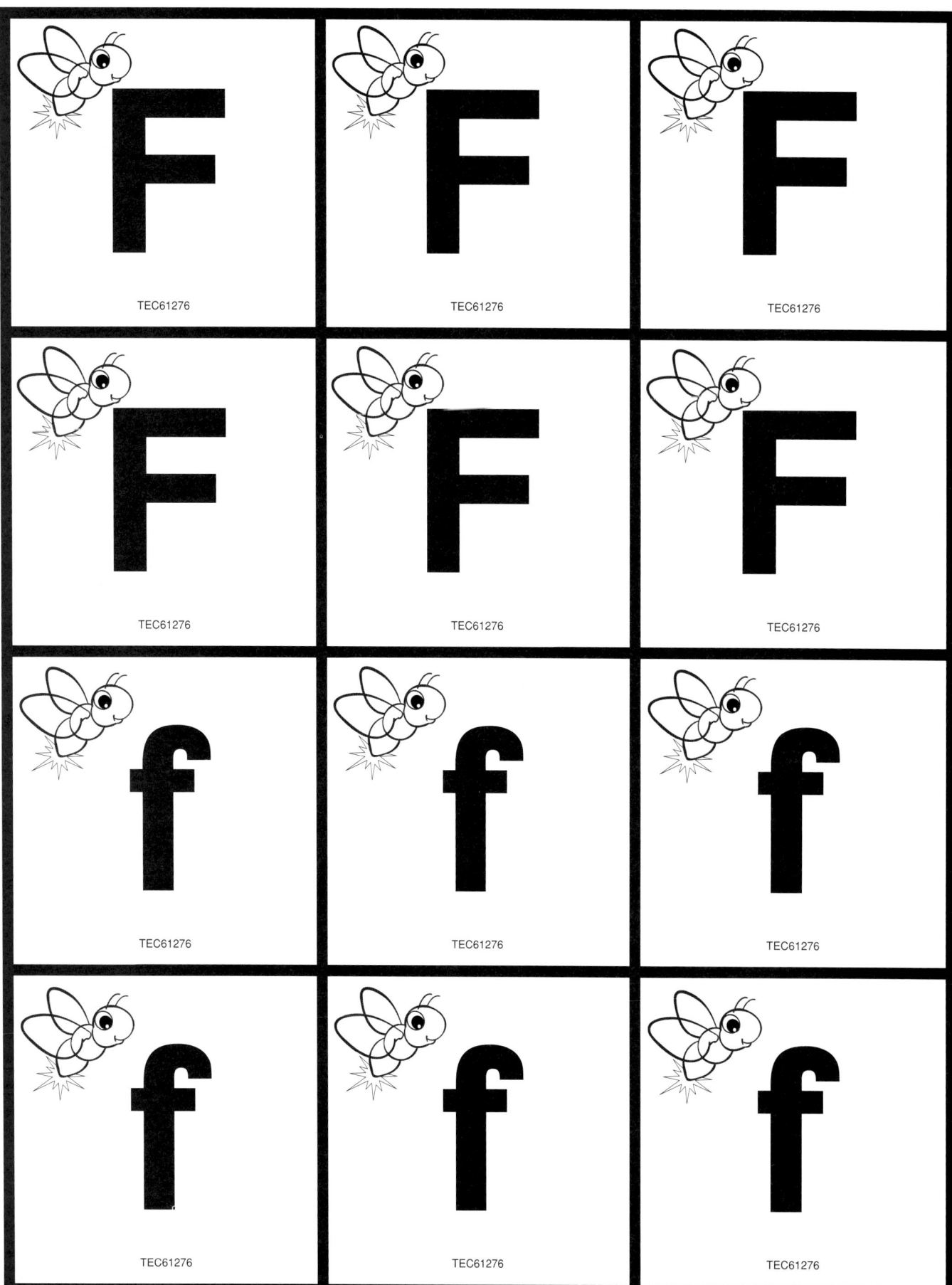

Beginning Sound Picture Cards Gg

Use with “Can You Find…” on page 29.

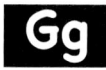

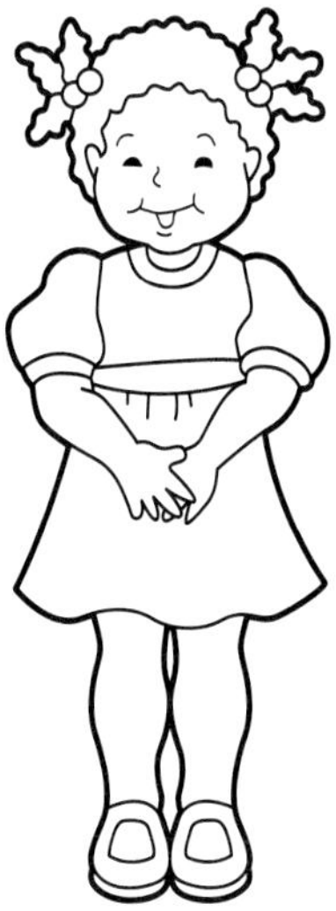

TEC61276

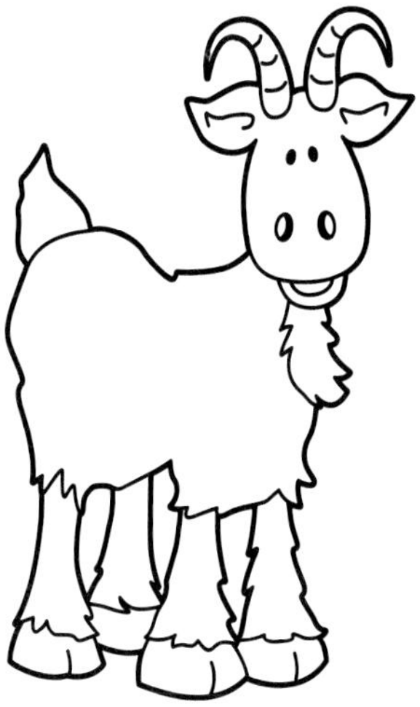

TEC61276

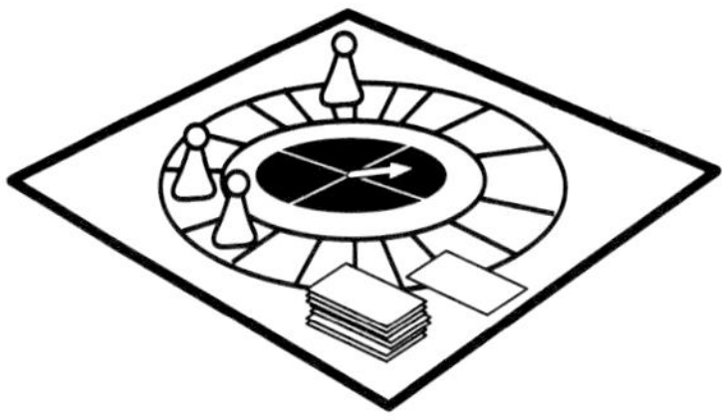

TEC61276

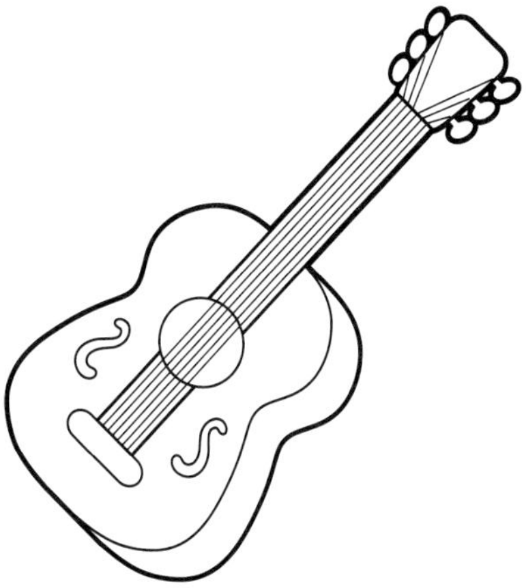

TEC61276

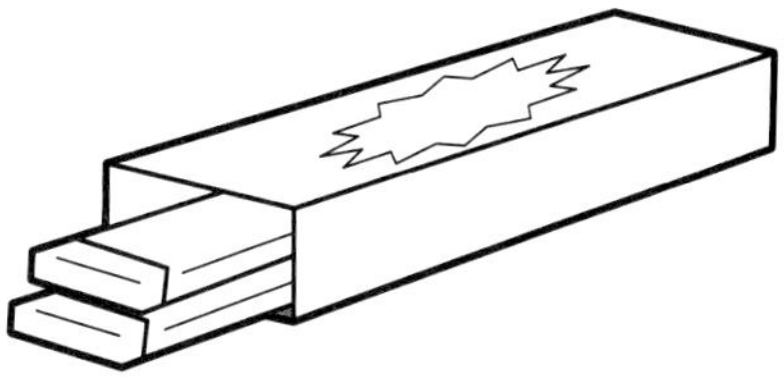

TEC61276

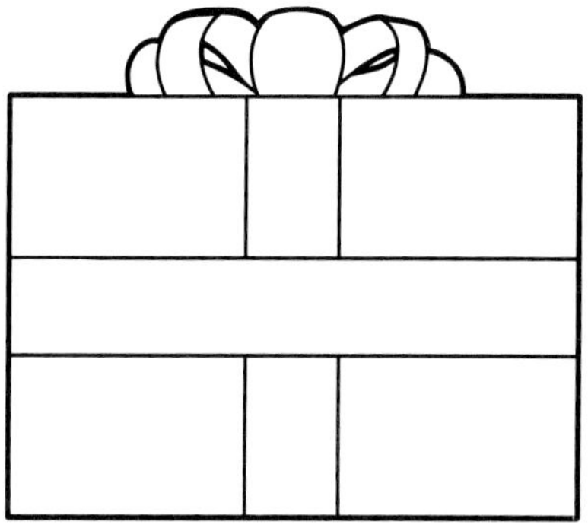

TEC61276

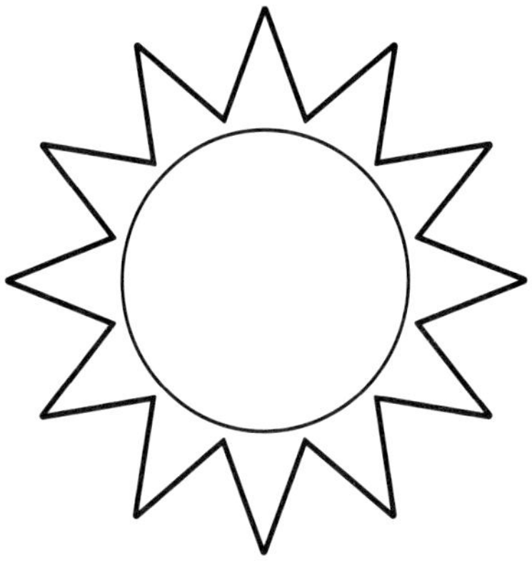

TEC61276

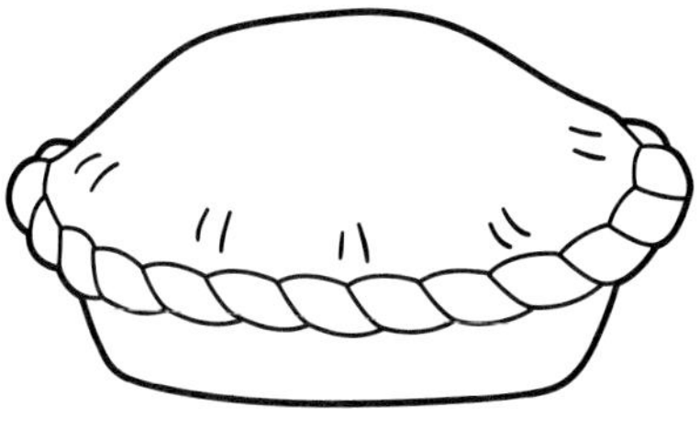

TEC61276

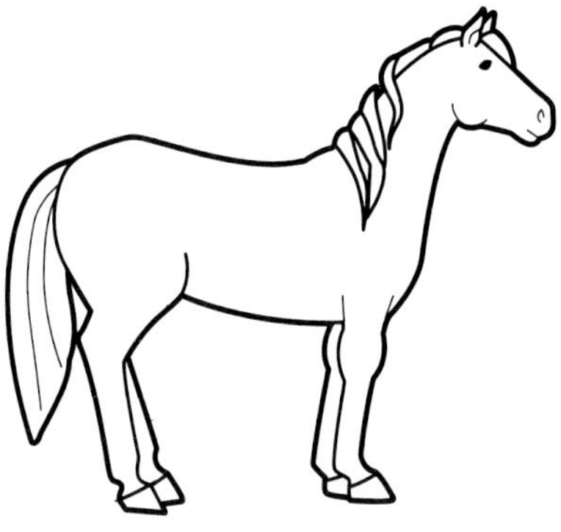

TEC61276

Gg Ending Sound Picture Cards
Use with "Does It End Like *Rug?*" on page 31.

Beginning Sound Picture Cards

Use with "Hay Is for Horses" on page 32 and "Hide-and-Seek" on page 33.

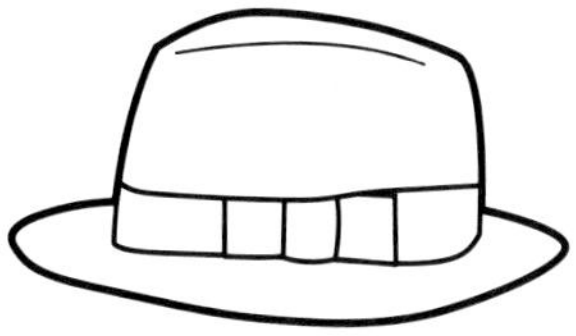

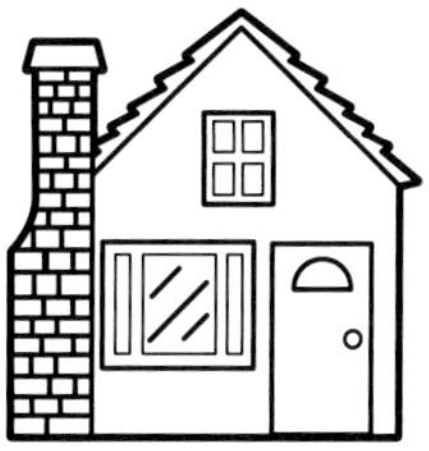

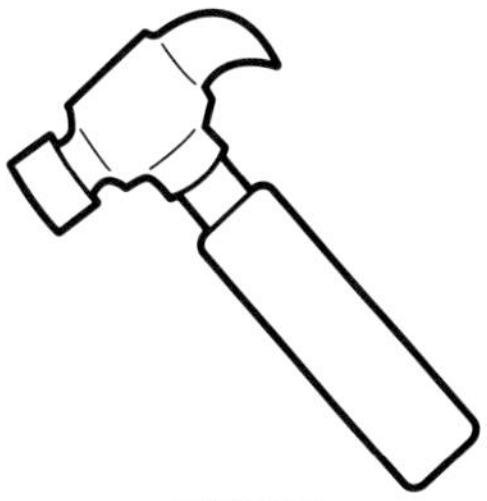

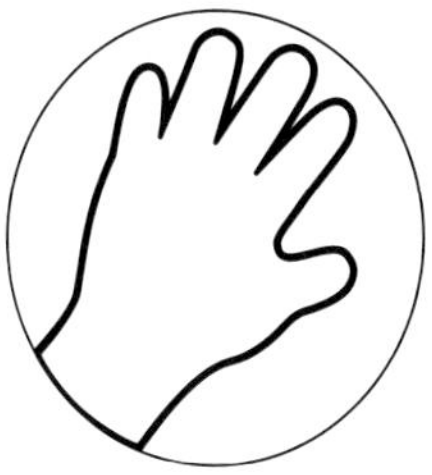

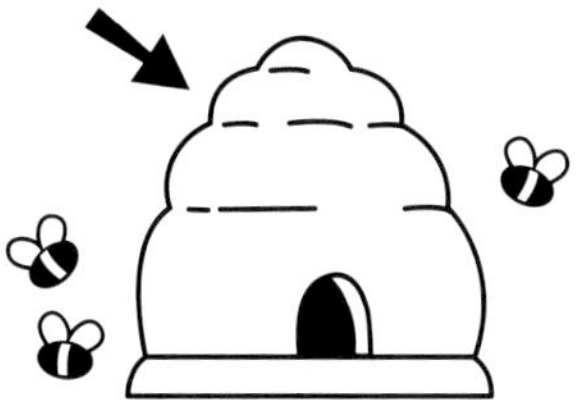

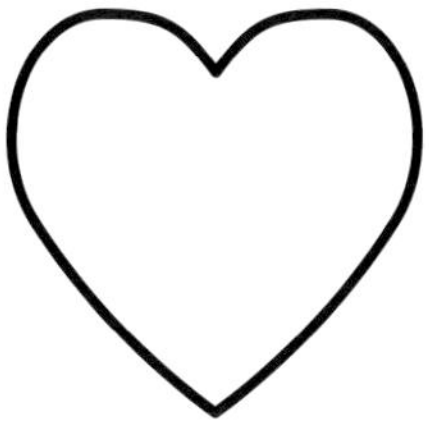

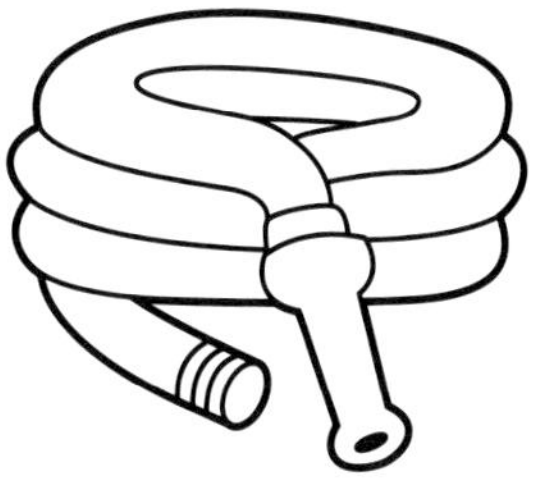

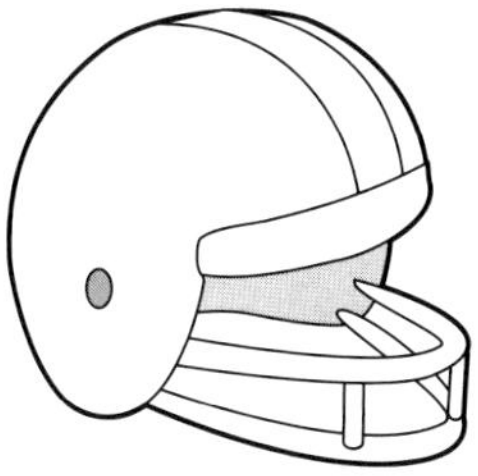

Horse Pattern

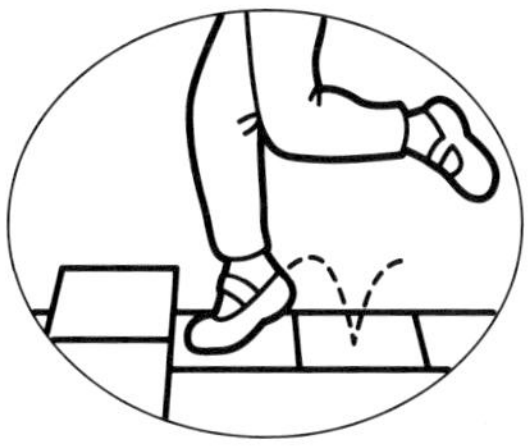

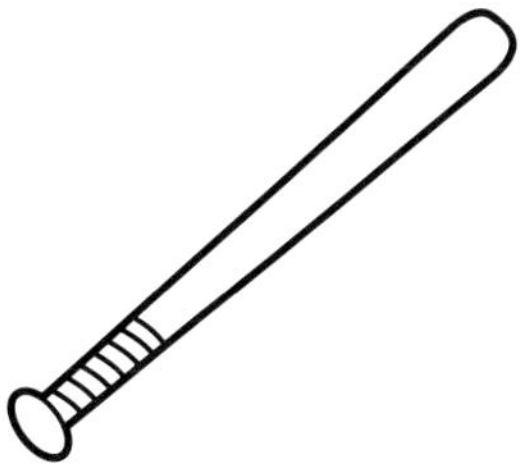

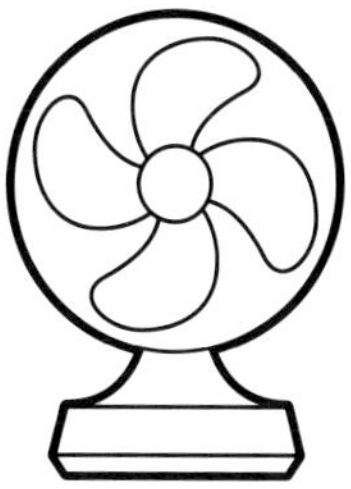

Use with "Hay Is for Horses" on page 32.

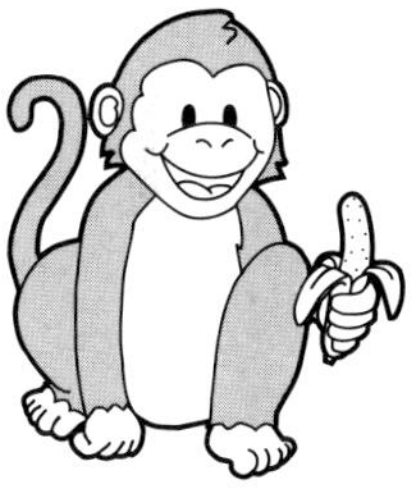

Kk **Key Patterns**
Use with "Lock and Keys" on page 46.

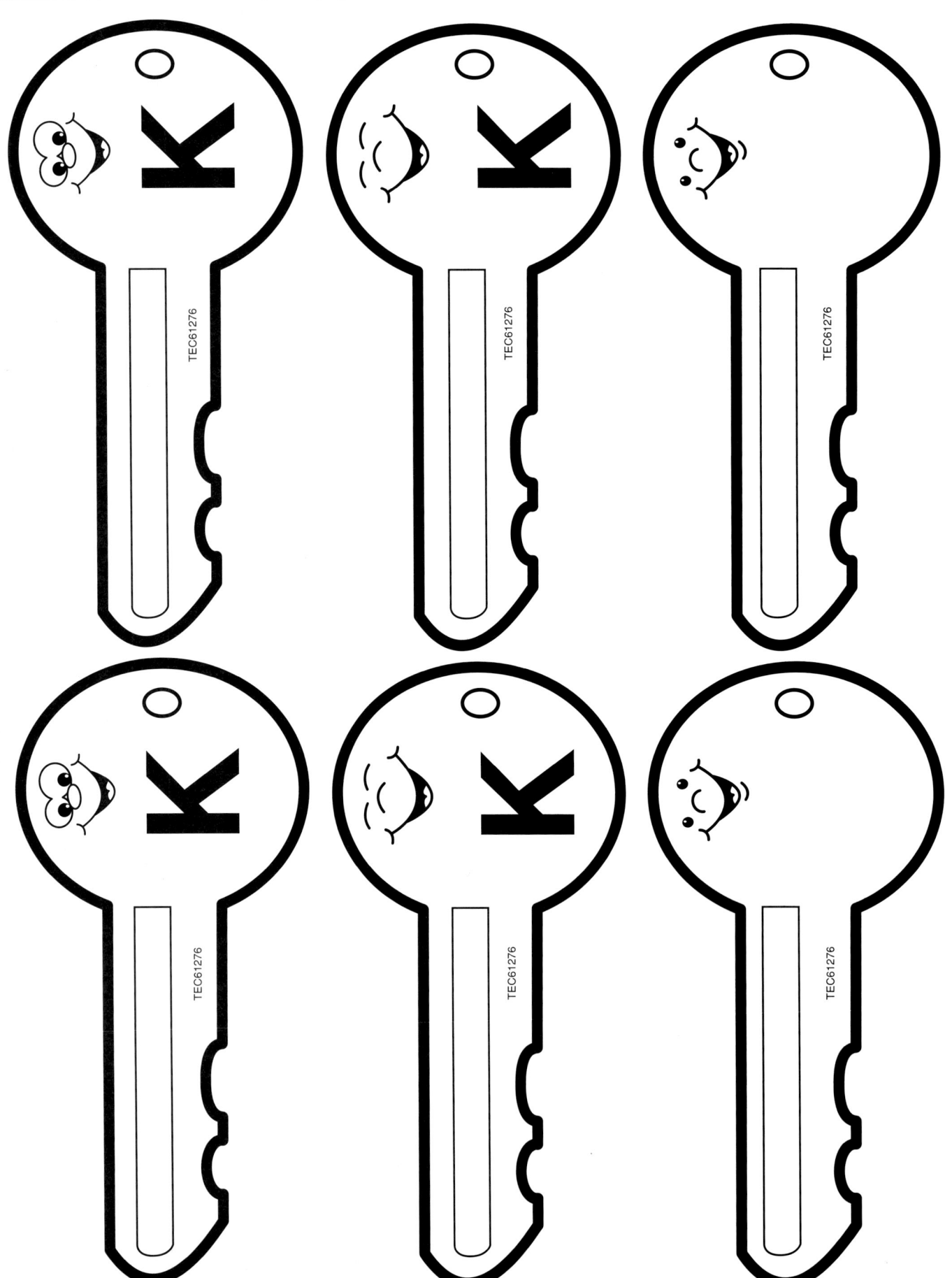

Picture Cards

Use with "What's for Lunch?" on page 48.

Ll

Nn **Picture Cards**
Use with "In the News" on page 56.

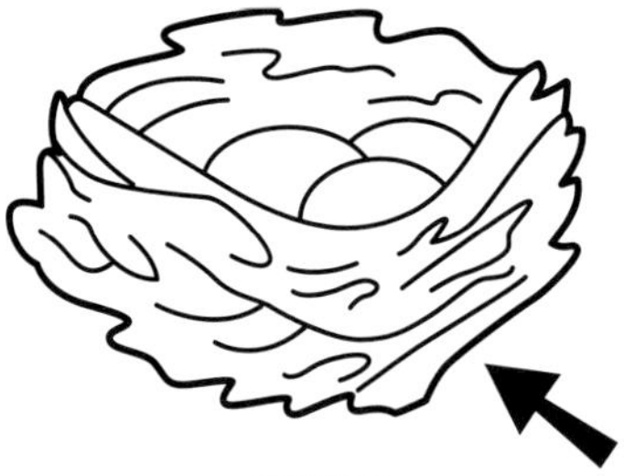

Nn **Noodle Patterns**
Use with "Noodle Soup" on page 59.

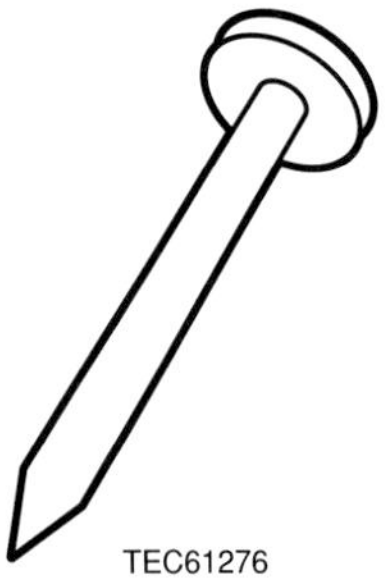

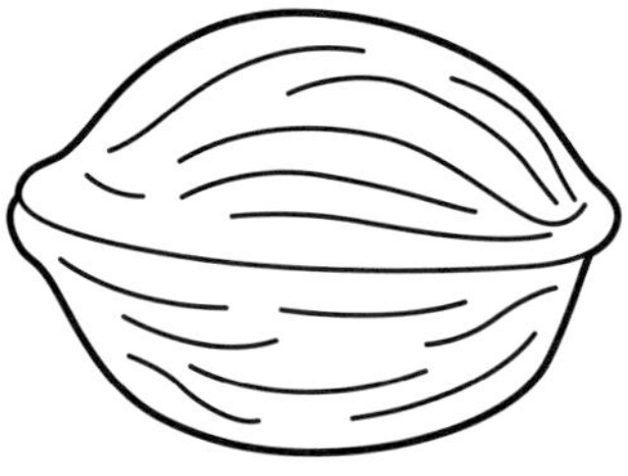

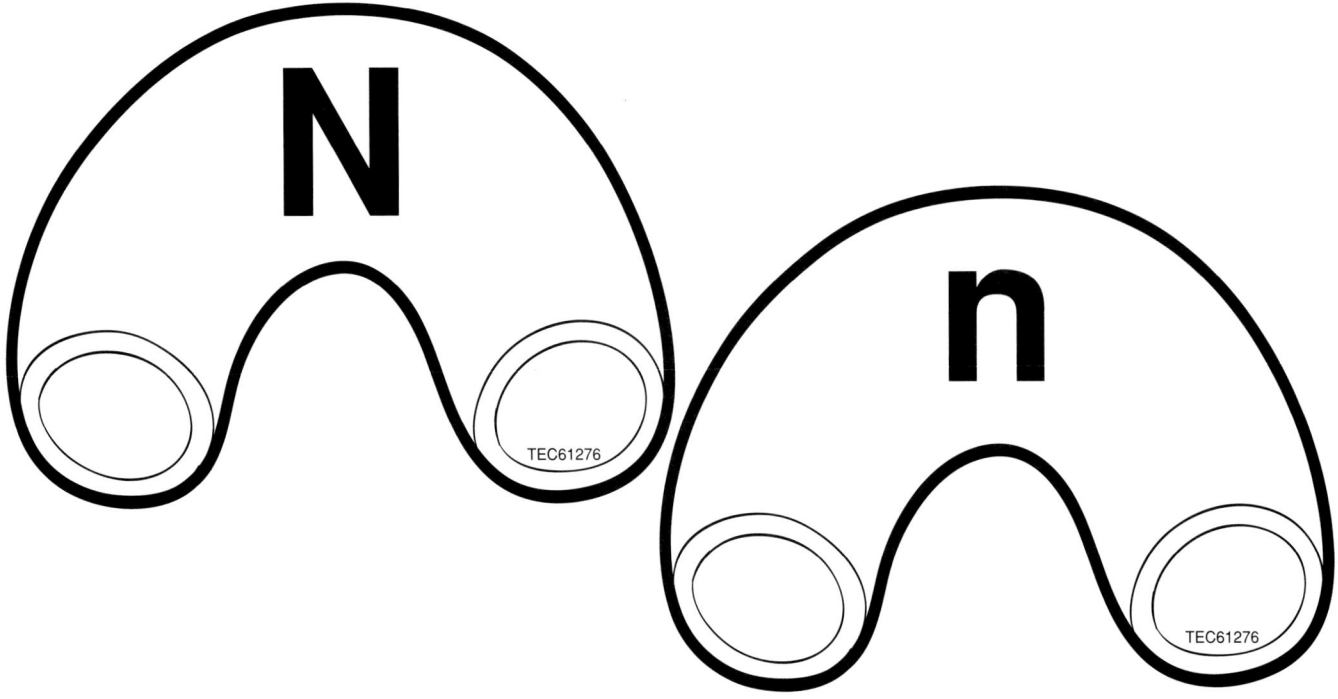

106 Circle Time From A to Z • ©The Mailbox® Books • TEC61276

Oo Medial Sounds Picture Cards
Use with "Sounds Like…" on page 63.

clock	frog	block
sock	dot	dog
pot	doll	top
pop	mop	fox
spot	lock	rock

Pepperoni Slices **Pp**

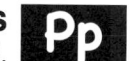

Use with "Pepperoni Pizza, Please" on page 64.

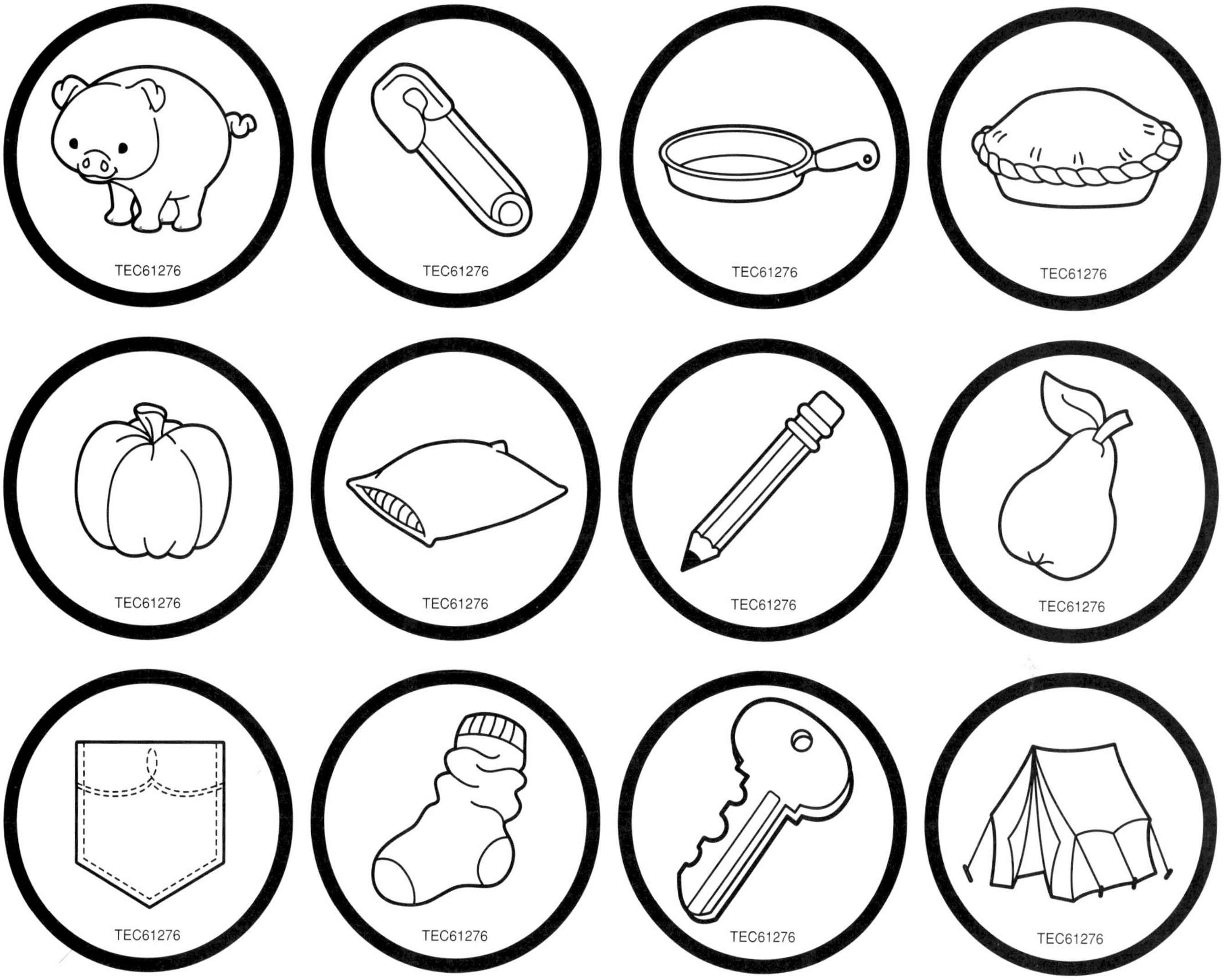

Pig Patterns **Pp**

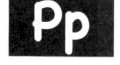

Use with "Pigs on the Loose" on page 67.

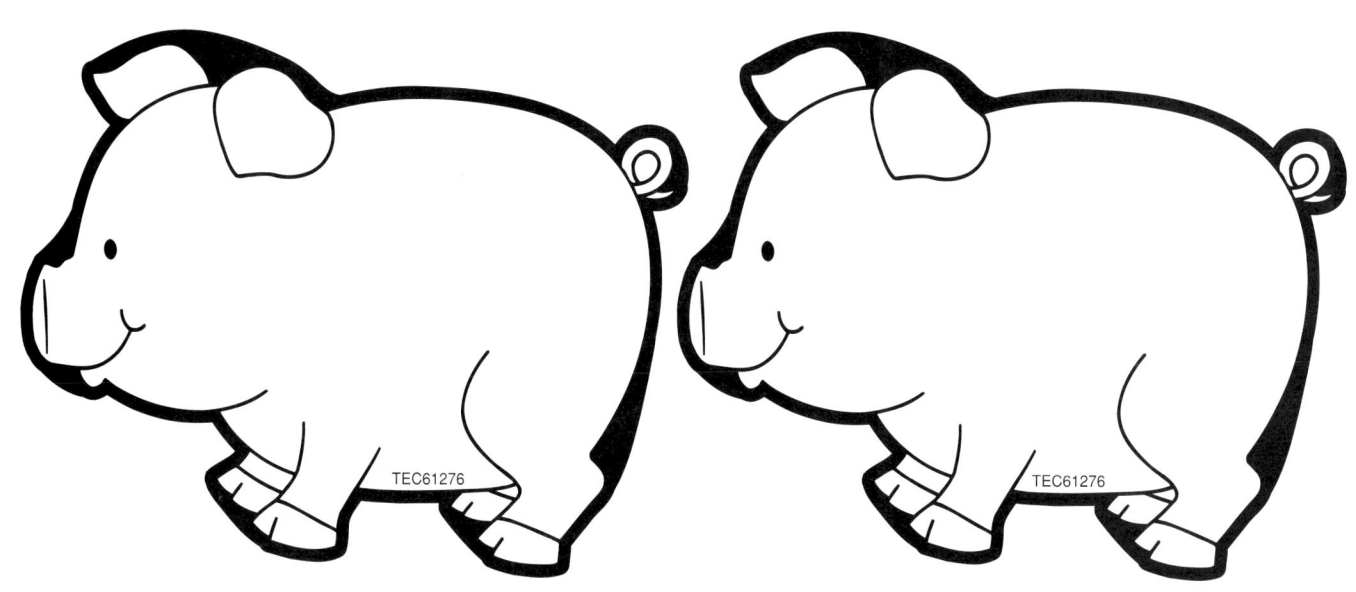

Rr Rose Cards
Use with "Rain on the Roses" on page 72.

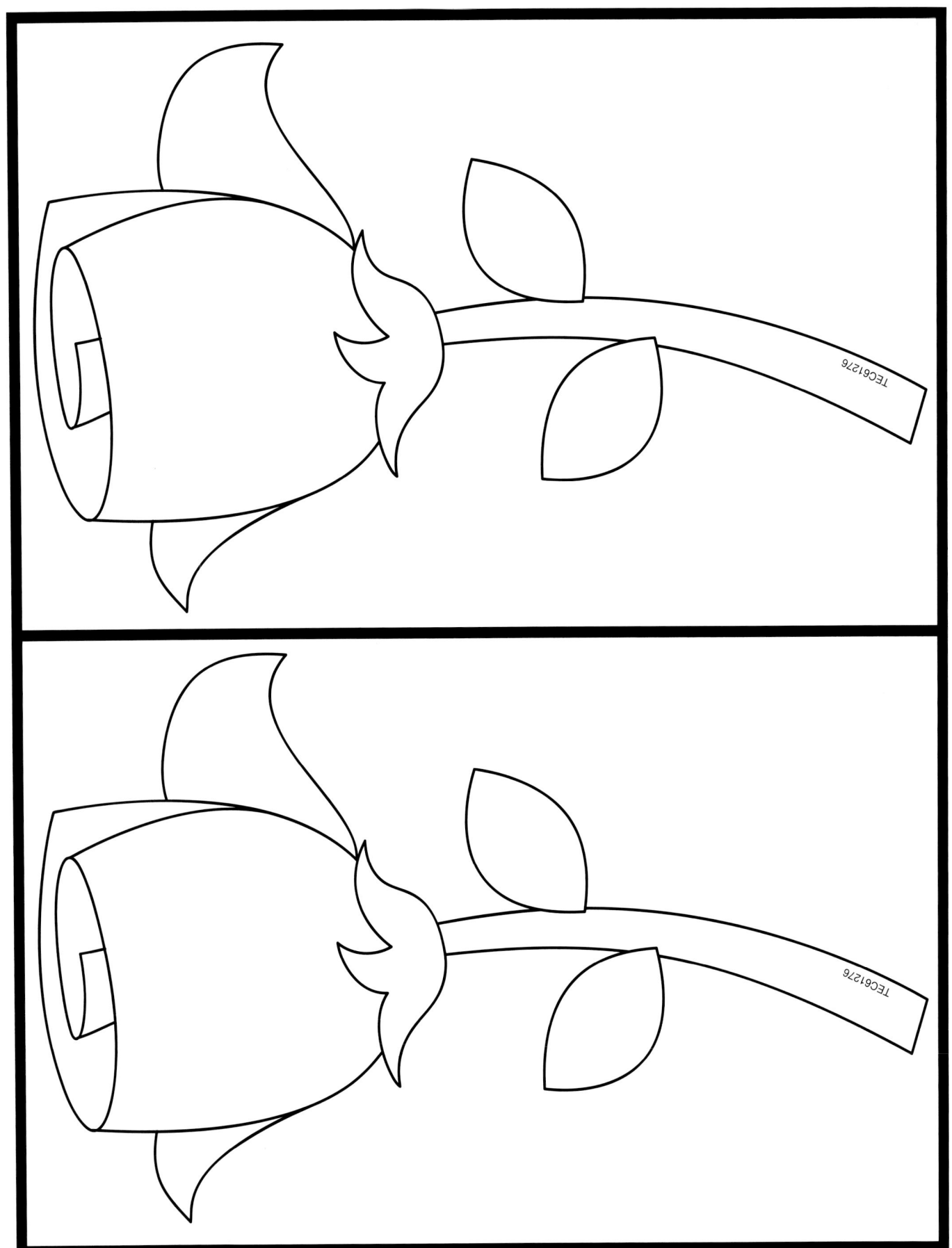

Beginning Sound Picture Cards
Use with "All Packed" on page 74.

Ss

Bb **Bee Patterns**
Use with "Busy Bees" on page 11.

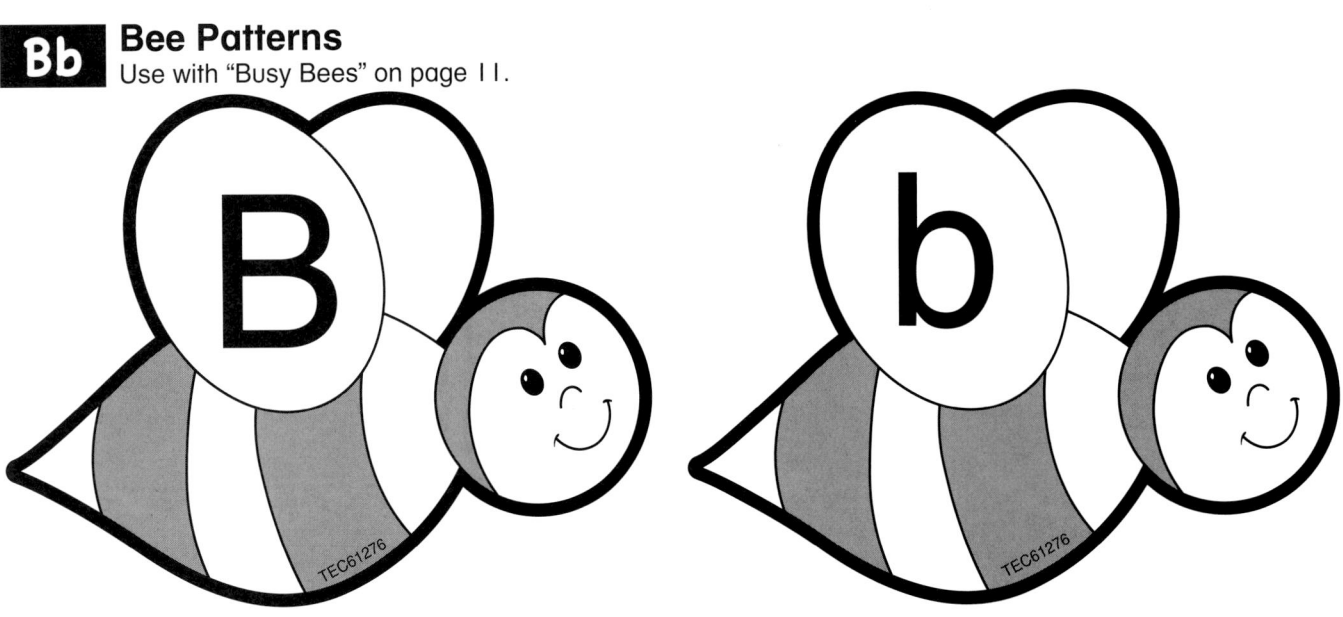

Ww **Beginning Sound Cards**
Use with "Wiggly Worms" on page 86.

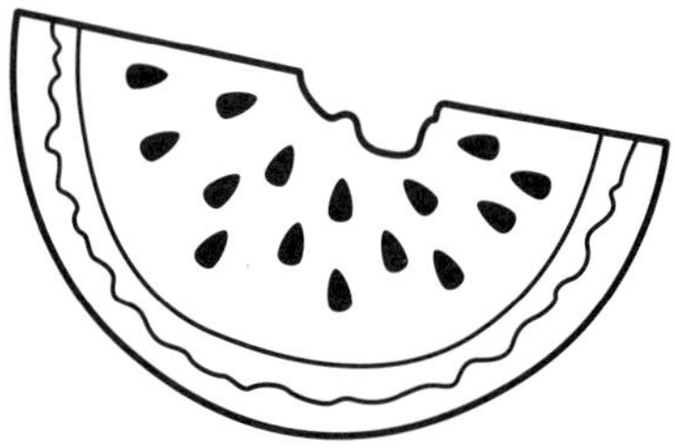

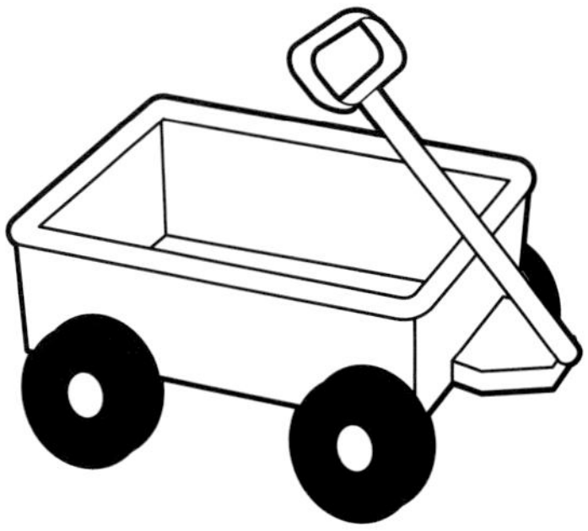

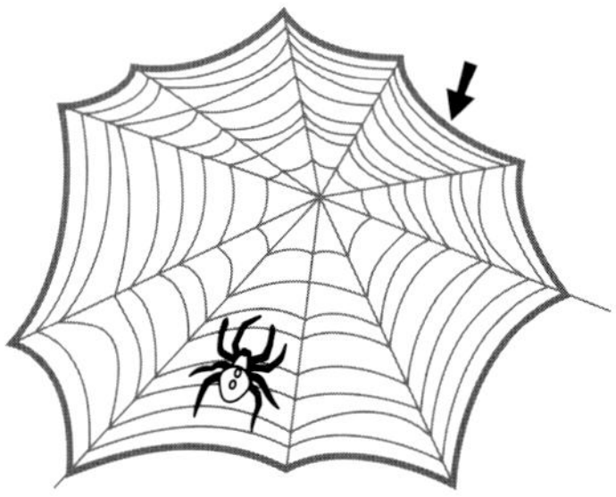

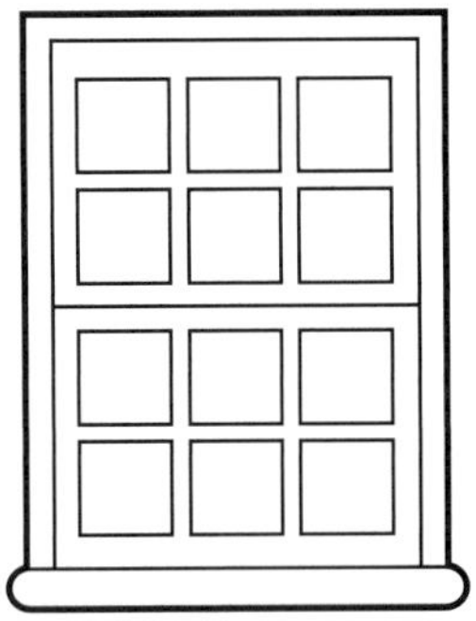

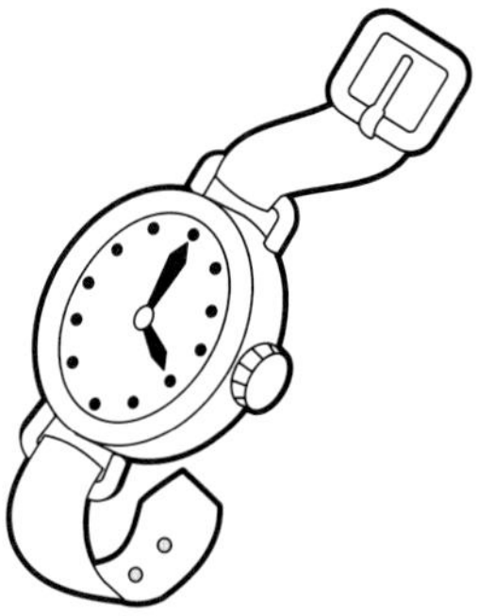

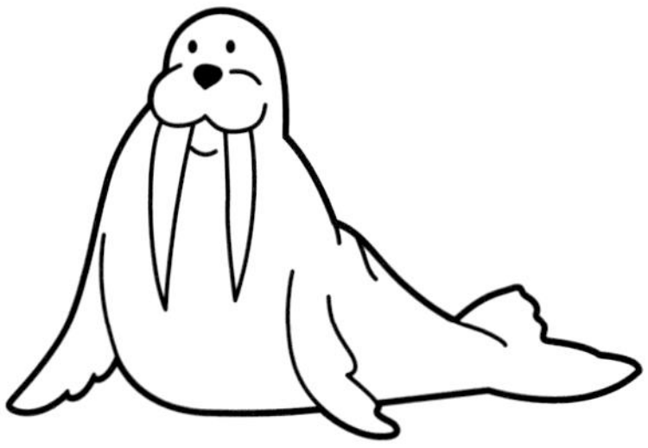

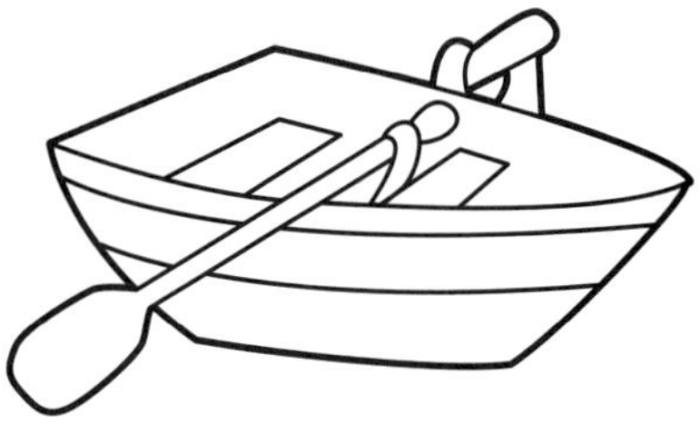

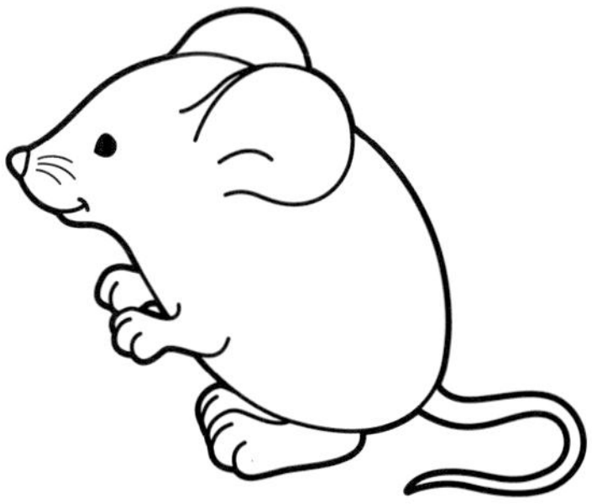

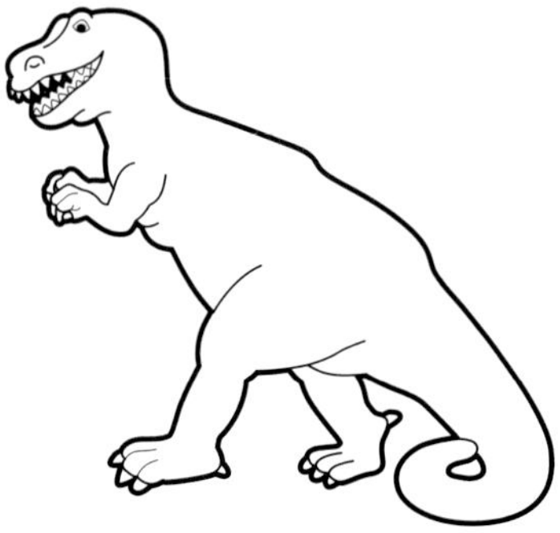